Soaring Above
The Problems
Of Life

*"They shall mount up
with wings as eagles."*
—ISAIAH 40:31

Jack Hartman

Library of Congress Catalog Card Number 86-81166

*"Thy Word is a lamp
unto my
feet, and a light
unto my path."*

PSALM 119:105

Published by:

 **LAMPLIGHT PUBLICATIONS**

P.O. Box 3293   Manchester, New Hampshire 03105

Designed and Produced by
Custom Graphics, Tulsa, Oklahoma

Contents

"The Lord gave the word and great was the company of those that published it" Psalm 68:11.

Introduction

It's obvious that there are many problems in this world. Our heavenly Father knows how to solve these problems. However, His ways are quite different from the ways of the world. "For My thoughts are not your thoughts, neither are your ways My ways, says the Lord. For as the heavens are higher than the earth, so are My ways higher than your ways, and My thoughts than your thoughts" (Isaiah 55:8-9, *AMP*).

Unfortunately, many Christians try to solve problems the way that the world solves problems. The world's ways are based on human logic and reasoning, but they are *spiritually dead*. "There is a way which *seemeth right* unto a man, but the end thereof are the ways of death" (Proverbs 14:12, *KJV*).

Many of the problems that we are faced with originate in the spiritual realm and must be solved in the spiritual realm. Human logic and reasoning cannot solve problems in the spiritual realm. In order to solve many of the problems that are giving us difficulty, we must learn the ways of God. "...the Lord knows how to rescue the godly out of temptations and trials..." (II Peter 2:9, *AMP*).

Our heavenly Father has given us the Holy Bible— His inspired Word—to tell us everything that any of us will ever need to know in order to solve our problems. As a result of dealing with problems in my own life and in the lives of many people whom I have counseled with, I have spent many years studying God's Word to see exactly what it says about how to solve problems. In this book I will share what I have learned during several years of study and application of these spiritual principles.

Every point that is made in this book will be thoroughly documented by Scripture. I pray that the following information will help many people to see God's ways of solving problems and to understand how different His ways are from the world's ways.

Chapter 1
Why Do We Have To Go Through Adversity?

Why is a child born with a horrible birth defect? Why is a beloved friend suddenly killed? Why is an innocent little girl sexually molested and raped? There are no "pat answers" to these and similar questions. There are many things that we'll never understand until we get to heaven. "...we can see and understand only a little about God now, as if we were peering at his reflection in a poor mirror; but someday we are going to see him in his completeness, face to face. Now all that I know is hazy and blurred, but then I *will* see everything clearly..." (I Corinthians 13:12, *TLB).*

Some of our problems obviously are beyond human comprehension, but many of our problems can be solved if we'll learn to react to them based upon the instructions in God's Word. It is full of instructions on how to deal with the adversity that *all* of us will face in our lives.

Jesus Christ experienced a great deal of adversity during His three-year earthly ministry. In fact, it is interesting to see that the Holy Spirit *actually led* Him into a period of trials and temptation at the very start of this ministry. "Then Jesus was led (guided) by the (Holy) Spirit into the wilderness (desert) to be tempted—that is, tested and tried—by the devil" (Matthew 4:1, *AMP).*

It is obvious that there was good to be found in Jesus' trial in the wilderness. Otherwise, the Holy Spirit never would have led Him into this period of testing. Jesus was tested and He passed. We also have to "pass tests" in order to grow and mature as Christians.

In our school days, we had to pass the tests that teachers gave us in order to pass courses and receive a promotion. The same principles apply in the spiritual realm. Our Father wants us to receive promotions. In order to receive them, we have to pass the tests of life.

What determines whether we pass or fail? The answer is the same in the spiritual realm as in the natural realm—it depends upon *how well we have done our homework.* Have we studied and meditated continually in God's Word? Have we learned what we need to learn in order to pass the tests? Have we obeyed these instructions?

Our heavenly Father wants us to be cleansed of sin. He wants us to be cleansed so that we will grow and mature and live our lives the way He wants us to live them. There are two ways to receive this cleansing: (1) by continual study and meditation in the Word of God and, (2) by going through the fires of adversity.

We have been given complete instructions in the Word of God. Everything we need to know is in this Book. If we study and meditate in it each day, it will cleanse us. "...Christ loved the church and gave Himself up for her, so that He might sanctify her, having *cleansed* her by the washing of the water with the Word..." (Ephesians 5:25-26, *AMP).*

Most of us enjoy taking a daily bath or a shower. It is relaxing and it cleanses our bodies. We also need to take a refreshing *spiritual* bath each day. This cleanses our *souls.* We do this by "soaking" ourselves each day in the Word of God — by saturating ourselves continually in it. Daily physical cleansing is good, but daily spiritual cleansing is much more beneficial. "Wherewith shall a young man *cleanse* his way? By taking heed and keeping watch [on himself] according to Your word [conforming his life to it]" (Psalm 119:9, *AMP*).

The cleansing power of God's Word can remove many impurities from our lives. However, if we refuse to pay the price of cleansing ourselves each day in God's Word, sooner or later these impurities will have to be *burned out* through the fires of adversity. Our heavenly Father is able to cleanse us no matter how badly we need cleansing. "...he is like a blazing fire refining precious metal and he can *bleach* the dirtiest garments! Like a refiner of silver he will sit and closely watch as the dross is *burned away*..." (Malachi 3:2-3, *TLB*).

If we react properly to problems, God will use this to cleanse us. This wonderful cleansing will reach deep down inside of us. "Blows that wound *cleanse* away evil, and strokes [for correction] reach to the *innermost* parts" (Proverbs 20:30, *AMP*).

Some people seem to go through one problem after another after another. This often is an indication that we aren't learning what we should learn from the problems that we are going through. What a tragic waste it is to go through all of the pain and suffering of a severe test only to fail and have to take it over again. **The worst tragedies are those tragedies from which no lessons are learned.**

If we react properly to problems, they will purify our faith and help it to grow. "These trials are only to test your faith, to see whether or not it is *strong* and *pure*. It is being tested as fire tests gold and purifies it — and your faith is far more precious to God than mere gold..." (I Peter 1:7, *TLB*).

Sometimes God has to let us get into a "pressure cooker" because this is the only way that many of us are going to grow. Steel is tempered and strengthened by fire. Christians often are tempered and strengthened by going through fiery trials and reacting properly based upon the instructions in God's Word.

When we're in the midst of the fires of adversity and refuse to waver in this test of our faith, we will meet the Lord Jesus who is there waiting for us. We can stand the heat because He is with us in the fire. We see a perfect example of this in the Biblical story of Shadrach, Meshach and Abednego.

King Nebuchadnezzar, a Babylonian king, had a large gold statue made. It was 90 feet high. He ordered his subjects to fall flat on the ground in front of the statue. If they didn't, they would be thrown into a fiery furnace.

Three young Jews — Shadrach, Meshach and Abednego — refused to worship this statue. They said, "If we are thrown into the flaming furnace, our God *is* able to deliver us..." (Daniel 3:17, *TLB)*. The king was furious. He commanded his soldiers to heat up the fire even more. The three young men were then tied up and thrown into the flames.

The Lord honored their faith. He met the three young men in the middle of the furnace and delivered them. "...suddenly, as he was watching, Nebuchadnezzar jumped up in amazement and exclaimed to his advisors, 'Didn't we throw three men into the furnace?' 'Yes,' they said, 'we did indeed, Your Majesty.' 'Well, look!' Nebuchadnezzar shouted. 'I see *four* men, unbound, walking around in the fire, and they *aren't* even hurt by the flames! And the fourth looks like *a god!*'" (Daniel 3:24-25, *TLB)*.

The king ordered the three young Jews to come out of the fire. "Then the princes, governors, captains and counselors crowded around them and saw that the fire *hadn't* touched them — not a hair of their heads was singed; their coats were unscorched, and they *didn't* even smell of smoke! Then Nebuchadnezzar said, 'Blessed be the God of Shadrach, Meshach and Abednego, for he sent his angel to deliver his trusting servants when they defied the king's commandment, and were willing to die rather than serve or worship any god except their own'" (Daniel 3:27-28, *TLB*).

Like these three young men, there are times in our lives when we have to walk in the fire — there is no alternative. When that happens, we can comfort ourselves with the fact that *the Lord is in there with us*. If we trust completely in Him, we will not be burned. "When thou passest through the waters, I *will* be with thee; and through the rivers, they shall *not* overflow thee: when thou walkest through the fire, thou shalt not be burned; *neither* shall the flame kindle upon thee" (Isaiah 43:2, *KJV*).

A refiner of silver and gold examines his precious metal very closely. He sits by the fire and watches carefully because he knows exactly how much heat is needed to remove the impurities. When we go through life's fiery trials, standing firmly and solidly on the Word of God, we will be refined and emerge like gold. "...he knows the way that I take; when he has tested me, *I will come forth as gold*" (Job 23:10, *NIV*).

Our heavenly Father knows just how much heat is needed to remove our impurities. He also knows how much we can take. As the fire grows hotter and hotter, more and more impurities are burned away. The precious metal remains the same. Only the waste material is removed. Each time we successfully go through a fiery trial, this tempers us, cleanses us and gives us more spiritual discipline to deal with future trials.

This process is similar to a potter molding clay. The potter kneads wet clay until air and excess water are removed. Then the clay pot is molded and left to dry. When the pot is dry, it is put into a kiln. If it is prepared properly, it will stand the test of the fire in the kiln. This is how our Father deals with us as we go through the fiery trials of life. "...as the clay is in the potter's hand, *so are you* in My hand..." (Jeremiah 18:6, *AMP*).

God is the Master Sculptor, the Potter. We are the clay. He knows *exactly* what is needed to mold us into the finished product that *He* wants us to become. We need to let go and let Him mold us *in the way He sees fit*. "Woe to the man who fights with his Creator. Does the pot argue with its maker? Does the clay dispute with him who forms it, saying, 'Stop, you're doing it wrong!'" or the pot exclaim, 'How clumsy can you be!'?" (Isaiah 45:9, *TLB*).

The problems in our lives enable us to grow. Our opportunity to grow is in direct proportion to the difficulty of the tests that we face. If we are able to comprehend this, we will face life's tests willingly, doing our very best to react to them in accordance with the instructions in God's Word. We should trust completely in our Father to use this positive reaction to a negative situation to continually mold us into the finished product that He wants us to become.

Chapter 2
The Blessings Of Adversity

As we go through life's trials and tribulations, we should realize that they often are used as a means of drawing us closer to the Lord. When we're chasing after pleasure it can be difficult to hear the Lord. Often, He can get our attention more readily when we're suffering and going through pain.

The crises in our lives often are signposts that direct us toward the Lord. Sometimes He has to allow crises to come up in our lives because of our ignorance of His Word and our failure to obey the instructions in His Word. If we violate God's laws, sooner or later this will cause us hardship and grief.

Whether we want to believe it or not, adversity is usually good for us. If we aren't living the way the Lord wants us to, sometimes He has to allow afflictions to come at us in given areas so we'll find out what His Word tells us to do and then obey His instructions. "Before I was afflicted I went astray, but *now Your word do I keep* [*hearing, receiving, loving and obey it*]" (Psalm 119:67, *AMP*).

If our troubles cause us to learn what God's Word says and to follow His instructions, this is good for us! It is much more beneficial to us than a large inheritance of money. "It is *good* for me that I was afflicted, that I may learn Thy statutes. The law of Thy mouth is *better* to me than thousands of gold and silver pieces" (Psalm 119:71-72, *NASV*).

Adversity can lead us in the direction we have to go in order to learn the truth we need to know.

Sometimes our Father has to allow Satan to get us in the darkness in order to find His light. Many of us would never learn His wonderful, precious Word if we didn't get into horrible, dreary situations where there didn't seem to be any relief. I can tell you from my personal experience and from the experiences of many of our Bible students that many of us never hear the Lord until we come upon a trying time in our lives — a time when we can't go any further with our human strength and abilities.

If this causes us to turn to the Word of God and study it diligently, we will see promises that we never knew were there. Even the promises that we know will be revealed in a new light. Afflictions often cause God's Word to *come alive* in our minds and hearts and *transform* our lives if we'll turn to it continually with humble trust and great hunger for its rich, magnificent truth.

Afflictions can cause us to learn many things about the ways of God. This knowledge will make us valuable workers for the kingdom of God. Our Father chooses His workers through affliction. "...I have chosen thee in the furnace of affliction" (Isaiah 48:10, *KJV*).

Our Father often has to discipline us before we can share in His holiness. It may seem difficult at the time but, if we react properly to this discipline, it will produce great blessings in due time. "Our fathers disciplined us for a little while as they thought best; but *God disciplines us for our good, that we may share in his holiness.* No discipline seems pleasant at the time, but painful. Later on, however, it produces a harvest of *righteousness* and *peace* for those who have been trained by it" (Hebrews 12:10-11, *NIV*).

The word "train" here means "to instruct" but it also can mean "to guide the growth of (a plant), as by tying, pruning..." according to *Webster's New World Dictionary*. This dictionary says that to "prune" is "to cut...to remove dead or living parts from (a plant) so as to increase fruit or flower production...to reduce or diminish by removing what is unnecessary."

Our heavenly Father is the great Pruner. He knows exactly where our "deadwood" is. He knows our bad traits that have to be cleaned out and He knows exactly how to do this without destroying the "plant" (us). Have you ever pruned a plant, a bush or a tree? Isn't it amazing how, when the "deadwood" is cleaned out, new growth appears? Pruning must be done carefully, but when it is done correctly, the results are excellent.

When a tree is pruned it may look ugly and bare at first, but great new life flows through it as a result of the pruning. This is how it is when the Master Pruner does a pruning job on us. It may not seem attractive at first, but if we react the way His Word tells us to react, new spiritual life will flow through us and glorious new fruit will be produced in our lives.

Our Father wants us to become more fruitful and, in His wisdom, He allows afflictions to come upon us for this reason. "...God hath caused me to be fruitful in the land of my affliction" (Genesis 41:52, *KJV*). When we get to the point where we start to produce some spiritual fruit, He prunes us repeatedly so that we will produce more and better fruit. "...He cleanses and repeatedly prunes every branch that continues to bear fruit, to make it bear more and richer and more excellent fruit" (John 15:2, *AMP*).

This verse shows us the correlation between pruning and cleansing. When our Father gently prunes us with His pruning knife, it may hurt for awhile but it actually cleanses us. He prunes us in love. Pruning is for our benefit. Pruning makes a vine stronger. If we react properly to God's pruning, it will make us stronger, too. We shouldn't be afraid of the pruning our Father will do. It will work out for the best. We *can* trust Him.

When too much "self" is in control of our lives, the Holy Spirit has to get out His pruning knife and do some cutting so we'll get out of the way and allow Him to produce His glorious fruit. He knows where we are weakest. He knows where we need to be pruned in order to increase strength in our weakest areas.

If we really trust in the Lord, we will be able to rejoice when we go through adversity because we *know* that He will strengthen us in our weakest areas. If we really do trust Him, we'll endure the pain as He prunes us, *knowing* that we'll be much better off after it is completed.

We see another example of how we can benefit from adversity in the way that oysters produce pearls. Pearls are precious gems which actually are a product of *pain*. When sand or some other foreign substance gets inside of an oyster's shell, it creates pain. The oyster reacts by producing a gummy substance to coat the irritating particle. This gummy substance produces a beautiful pearl — a precious gem that would *not* have been produced *without pain.*

The same principle applies in our lives. Just as pearls are produced through an oyster's pain, our Father can create a "pearl" from our adversities if we surrender to Him with complete trust. A life of continuous pleasure and ease is like quicksand—it will eventually pull us under. We *need* to face adversity in our lives. If we learn how to respond to adversity based upon God's Word, this is good for us, not bad.

Many things that seem bad to us are *good* in God's

eyes and many things that seem good to us are *bad* from His viewpoint. He can see so much that we can't see. We see trials. God sees blessings. He knows that the problems that we face often are the greatest things that could happen to us.

We are inclined to conclude too much based upon what we see and hear and how we feel. God knows so much more. Often He is working behind the scene in ways that we can't even begin to comprehend. Many times when everything seems bad, He is actually preparing to bless us abundantly if we'll just hold fast and refuse to waver one bit from the instructions He has given in His Word. Our Father risks allowing problems to break us down because He wants to use them to build us up if we'll just react to them the way that His Word instructs us to react to them.

Sometimes the problems in our lives end up bringing about the answers to our prayers. If we react properly to these problems, our Father often will turn them into blessings that will be the answer to the prayers that we have asked of Him. Often we pray to God for *relief* from certain problems when we should be praying for His wisdom and His strength to bring us *through* these problems to the blessings that He has for us on the other side.

Someday when we're in heaven we'll see that many of the greatest blessings in our lives were available to us based upon our reaction to what seemed to be our biggest problems. We'll also see that relatively small problems in our lives on earth could have won us glorious eternal rewards if we had reacted to them based upon the instructions that we have been given in God's Word.

Many of the seemingly worst problems here on earth contain a tremendous opportunity for eternal gain — a blessing that we'll enjoy for endless trillions

19

of years in heaven in exchange for responding properly to a few months or years of adversity here on earth. "These troubles and sufferings of ours are, after all, quite *small* and *won't* last very long. *Yet this short time of distress will result in God's richest blessing upon us forever and ever!*" (II Corinthians 4:17, *TLB*).

We need to realize that God hides treasure in the midst of every problem. Will we look for the treasure? Will we find it? Or, will we be so preoccupied with the problem that we miss the treasure that God has hidden in the center??

When everything seems dark, we often can't see the bright light of God with our limited human vision. "...men *see not* the bright light which is in the clouds..." (Job 37:21, *KJV*). We look at the clouds from the bottom. God looks down from the top. He sees them from an entirely different perspective than we do.

When the cloudy, stormy days of life come upon us, this is when we are most likely to experience the glory of the Lord *if* we react to the adversity the way His Word tells us to react. "...behold, the glory of the Lord *appeared in the cloud*" (Exodus 16:10, *KJV*).

Adversity often causes us to seek the Lord, and as we draw closer to Him, He draws closer to us. "Come close to God and He will come close to you..." (James 4:8, *AMP*). *How can anything be bad if it causes us to draw closer to the Lord and Him to draw closer to us???* It is much, much better to go through the storms of life with a close personal relationship with Jesus Christ than it is to go through smooth sailing without Him.

Many times the storms of life blow us right into the arms of the Lord. When we can't go any further, He catches us and holds us fast. "The eternal God is your refuge, and underneath are the everlasting arms..." (Deuteronomy 33:27, *NIV*). He is always there and He'll always catch us if we trust Him. Each time we let go of our fears and trust Him to catch us, we'll grow that much closer to Him. Many people (myself included) can look back at days of despair with great joy in the realization that this hardship led to a much closer walk with the Lord.

Our Father has many blessings that can only be received if we'll draw close to Him. Our problems often become a time of revelation to us, revealing Him to us in a beautiful way that we couldn't see otherwise. We draw close to Him in the bad times because we develop a joy that is much deeper and much richer than anything this world has to offer. "Sorrow is *better* than laughter, for by the sadness of the countenance the heart is made *better* and *gains gladness*" (Ecclesiastes 7:3, *AMP*).

Many times our Father has to allow problems to come into our lives in order to break down the pride that He sees in us. Sometimes we need to be broken before He can put us back together again. He withholds blessings from proud people and gives blessings to the humble.

Our Father is in complete control. No problems can come into our lives without His permission. God and love are one and the same. "...*God is love*" (I John 4:8, *KJV*). Would a loving God allow problems to come into our lives if they couldn't be beneficial in this life and for our eternal benefit after we leave this earth???

Our Father will never allow anything to happen to us that wouldn't be good for us over the long haul. He allows problems to come into our lives to make us *better*, not *bitter*. If we are resentful because of our problems, then we obviously haven't learned what He wants us to learn.

We should always *look for the blessing* that is contained in each problem. If we do and if we react to each problem according to the instructions in God's Word, we'll continually turn life's problems into blessings here on earth and throughout eternity.

Chapter 3
The Growth Of Character And Maturity Through Adversity

Our Father didn't create us just so that we could have fun, pleasing ourselves, doing what we want to do. He put us here to grow, develop and mature so that we could find His will for our lives and fulfill it. From His point of view, trials and tribulations can cause us to grow spiritually when nothing else will.

One of the blessings of successfully dealing with trials and tribulations is the development of *character*. God's Word says that character is developed by going through trials and maintaining faith and patience in God. "We can *rejoice*, too, when we run into problems and trials for we know that they are good for us — they help us learn to be *patient*. And patience develops *strength of character* in us and helps us *trust God more* each time we use it until finally our hope and faith are *strong* and *steady*" (Romans 5:3-4, *TLB*).

This is a very interesting verse of Scripture. It starts out by telling us to rejoice when we run into problems. This is just the opposite of our natural inclination. When we run into problems our natural inclination is to grumble, complain and feel sorry for ourselves.

Why does God's Word tell us to rejoice? We are told to rejoice because, if we react to these problems the way that God's Word tells us to react, we will, (a) become more patient, (b) develop strength of character and, (c) develop our faith so that it is strong and steady.

Steel receives its temper from fire. Precious gems are made into jewels by grinding. Problems are the structural steel that our Father uses to build character. This character is developed by going through adversities, finding our Father's great truths and applying them with strong, unwavering, persevering faith.

Character cannot be developed without pain. We all know people of great character, and every one of these people has been through many problems in their lives. Many of us look for the easy way out, but we don't develop character by trying to evade problems. This is what our carnal nature wants, but this isn't God's way. Character is developed by facing our problems head on and dealing with them according to the instructions in our Father's Word.

No one had greater character than Jesus Christ. His perfect character was not developed in easy times—He became a leader because of the problems that He had to endure. *"...his suffering made Jesus a perfect Leader..."* (Hebrews 2:10, *TLB*).

Our Father allows us to suffer through trials and tribulations so that we can develop the character and strength that He wants us to develop. *"...after you have suffered a little while*, the God of all grace — Who imparts all blessing and favor — Who has called you to His [own] eternal glory in Christ Jesus, *will Himself complete and make you what you ought to be*, establish and ground you securely, and strengthen (and settle) you"* (I Peter 5:10, *AMP*).

It's interesting to see that God Himself will complete us and make us what He wants us to be. When will He do this?? He'll do it after we have suffered awhile (and reacted to this suffering in accordance with the instructions in His Word).

Skillful sailors never learn their skill on a calm

sea. It is developed by going through storms and learning how to sail in the midst of them. We cannot grow and mature in character without going through problems. We have to get out of the safe harbor and into the storms. As we do this repeatedly, we will mature and grow and the storms of life will affect us less and less. Once we successfully come through a number of storms with the Lord, what are a few more of the same???

With every surmounted obstacle, we grow a little more in faith and character. When the pressure is intense, we have the opportunity to learn great and lasting truths from God's Word that will not only pull us through the current problems but also stand us in good stead for the rest of our lives.

The lessons we learn from the hard times today give us a solid foundation for all of the tomorrows that are ahead of us. If we react to hard times the way that our Father wants us to react, He will cause us to grow and mature. "...O God of my righteousness: thou hast *enlarged me* when I was in distress..." (Psalm 4:1, *KJV*).

We need to get out of our comfortable ruts if we're going to grow. We see a good example of this with a mother eagle and her baby eaglet. The baby wants to stay in the nest where it's warm and comfortable and all food is provided. However, the mother knows when it's time for the baby to leave. When this time comes, the mother shakes the nest until the baby eaglet falls out. When the little eaglet is falling through the air, instinctively flapping its little wings, the mother eagle is right there watching closely.

When the eaglet can't fly any further, the mother flies underneath and catches the baby on her great wings. After a while she lets him go again and lets him fly a little more before catching him again. This is the way that an eagle learns to fly. The Bible explains that God works with us in the same way.

He allows problems to come into our lives to stop us from "hiding out" in our "nests." When we're out there "flapping around" and we can't go any further on our own strength, He is there. He will catch us. He won't let us fall. "He spreads his wings over them, even as an eagle overspreads her young. She carries them upon her wings—*as does the Lord his people!*" (Deuteronomy 32:11, *TLB*).

Growth is possible in the midst of adversity, but it is *not* automatic. Many people go through adversity and don't grow in the least. What is it that determines who grows and who doesn't? The answer is found in one word — *obedience*. The Christian who grows in the midst of adversity is the Christian *who finds out* what God says to do and then *obeys* these instructions. The Christian who doesn't grow in the midst of adversity either doesn't know what God says to do or knows but doesn't obey these instructions.

Jesus is our role model. Even He had to go through difficult times in order to learn obedience. "*Although He was a Son, He learned obedience from the things which He suffered*" (Hebrews 5:8, *NASV*). If Jesus Christ had to go through hard times in order to learn obedience, *why* would any of us think we are any different???

When trials come at us, we need to turn to the Lord, listen to His instructions and obey them. If we do our part, He will not let us down. "When you are in tribulation, and all these things come upon you in the latter days, *if* you *turn to* the Lord your God, and are *obedient* to His voice, for the Lord your God is a merciful God, *He will not fail you...*" (Deuteronomy 4:30-31, *AMP*).

If we'll do exactly what God tells us to do, then *He*

Himself will stand firmly against whatever is coming against us. "...if you will indeed *listen to* and *obey* His voice and all that I speak, then *I* will be an enemy to your enemies and an adversary to your adversaries" (Exodus 23:22, *AMP).*

When we are at our weakest and it doesn't seem as though we can take one more step, God watches to see if we obey His instructions. If we faithfully obey them, He will rescue us from our seemingly hopeless trials:

"He reached down from heaven and took me and *drew me out* of my great trials. He *rescued me* from deep waters. He *delivered me* from my strong enemy, from those who hated me — I who was helpless in their hands. On the day when I was weakest, they attacked. But *the Lord held me steady. He led me to a place of safety,* for he delights in me. The Lord rewarded me *for doing right* and being pure. For *I have followed his commands* and have *not* sinned by turning back from following him. *I kept close watch on all his laws;* I did *not* refuse a single one. *I did my best to keep them all,* holding myself back from doing wrong. *And so the Lord has paid me with his blessings,* for I have done what is right, and I am pure of heart. This he knows, for he watches my every step" (Psalm 18:16-24, *TLB).*

These verses of Scripture are extremely comforting. If we'll do our part, the Lord will do His part. What is our part? Our part is to follow the instructions in His Word to the very best of our ability. If we will do this and persevere, the Lord will do His part. His part is to rescue us from our trials and to deliver us from strong enemies. Even when we are helpless and at our weakest, He will help us.

Many of us do not find solutions to our problems because we don't pay the price to, (a) learn what God's

Word says and, (b) to obey His instructions. Again and again God's Word tells us that He *will* bless us and solve our problems *if* we will seek Him with all our hearts and do exactly what His Word tells us to do. The more our thoughts, words and actions line up with His Word, the less room we give Satan to get a foothold and the more we give God the channel through which He will bless us.

Our Father will never force His will on us. He gave all of us complete freedom of choice. He wants very much to bless us, but we must willingly choose to learn and obey the instructions that He has given us. If we'll pay careful attention to what He says and follow the paths that He tells us to follow, He will guide us every step of the way:

"Listen, my son, *accept* what I say, and the years of your life will be *many*. I guide you in the way of *wisdom* and lead you along *straight paths*. When you walk, your steps will *not* be hampered; when you run, you will *not* stumble. *Hold on to instruction, do not let it go; guard it well, for it is your life*" (Proverbs 4:10-13, *NIV*).

We can see the tremendous emphasis that God's Word places on following His instructions. We don't automatically receive God's blessings here on earth just because we are Christians. Blessings are automatic in heaven, but not here on earth. We need to find the instructions that He has given in His Word and cheerfully obey them. If we do this, He will help us. "*You come to the help of those who gladly do right, who remember your ways*" (Isaiah 64:5, *NIV*).

Our Father has tremendous blessings for us. We receive these blessings through trust and obedience —by trusting Him completely and by following His instructions exactly. When we do this, He'll take good care of us. "...*if we obey him, everything will turn out well for us*" (Jeremiah 42:6, *TLB).*

Many of our Father's promises are conditional. He will always do His part. Will we do ours??? When we do what the Word of God tells us to do, we can count on Him to do what His Word says He will do. He wants to bless us with every promise in His Word and He will if we'll obey His instructions and do our very best to live our lives the way that His Word tells us to.

If we do this, we'll have fewer problems and we'll get over the ones we do have much more rapidly. Our Father is looking for our willing compliance to His will instead of stubborn insistence on doing our will. "I *will* instruct you and teach you in the way you should go; I *will* counsel you and watch over you. Do *not* be like the horse or the mule, which have no understanding but must be controlled by bit and bridle or they will not come to you" (Psalm 32:8-9, *NIV).*

When a pilot can't see, he flies by instruments. He trusts completely in them and disregards his natural inclinations to fly in a certain direction. When our lives seem to be upside down and the problems have us completely befuddled and we don't know which way to turn, we also need to "fly by instruments" —by the instructions in God's Word. Even if they seem wrong to us, we need to trust completely in them.

When we can't see the way, our Father can. He'll pull us through if we trust the wisdom of His wonderful Word. "Lay hold of my words with *all* your heart; *keep* my commands and you *will* live. *Get* wisdom, *get* understanding; do *not* forget my words or swerve from them. Do *not* forsake wisdom, and she *will* protect you; *love her*, and she *will* watch over you" (Proverbs 4:4-6, *NIV).*

The adversities in our lives can cause us to grow and mature tremendously *if* we respond correctly to them. If we follow our Father's specific instructions, we will come out on top and we'll be better off for having gone through the adversity.

Chapter 4
How Should We React To Adversity?

Many Christians who have been reborn spiritually still react to adversity the same way that non-Christians react. This is not what our heavenly Father wants us to do. He has given us specific instructions showing us exactly how He wants us to react to adversity. If we react the way that His Word tells us to, we will be blessed. The effect that our problems have upon us is largely determined by what we do with the instructions that our Father has given to us.

When God created us, He didn't want a bunch of robots, so He gave each of us the power to choose. All day long, every day of our lives, all of us use this power of choice to decide what we think, what we believe, what we say, what we do and how we react to different situations.

If we decide the way that God's Word tells us to decide, His light will shine on what we do. "What you decide on will be done, and light will shine on your ways" (Job 22:28, *NIV*). If we don't make the choice to obey God's Word, we're going to have to pay the penalty for this decision. "...you *closed your eyes* to the facts and *did not choose* to reverence and trust the Lord, and you *turned your back* on me, *spurning* my advice. That is why you must eat the bitter fruit of *having your own way*, and experience the full terrors of the pathway you have chosen" (Proverbs 1:29-31, *TLB*).

Too often we disregard God's Word and make the choice that *seems right* to us. This is wrong and it doesn't meet with His approval. "...I spoke but you did *not* listen. You did evil in my sight and *chose* what *displeases* me" (Isaiah 65:12, *NIV)*. Our Father has given us the right to choose to do whatever we want to do, but if our decisions are based upon ignorance of or disobedience to the instructions in His Word, we must face the consequences.

Life is a series of choices. We continually come to crossroads and must decide to go in one direction or another. Satan wants us to take the wide road — the way that seems easy to us. God wants us to take the narrow road — the road that His Word says to take *whether or not it makes sense to our limited, finite minds*. The cumulative result of the continual series of choices that each of us makes is the most important factor in determining the quality of our lives.

Long ago, I learned a very important truth — *the important thing in life is not what happens to us, but how we react to what happens to us*. Two people can be faced with the same problem and many times one person will react much differently from the other. Why is this?

The varied reactions are caused by the difference in what those people believe deep down in their hearts. The apostle Paul said, "...I have *learned* how to be *content* (satisfied to the point where I am *not* disturbed or disquieted) in *whatever* state I am" (Philippians 4:11,*AMP)*. It's interesting to see that Paul said he has *learned* this.

We don't have to react negatively every time a problem comes upon us. *We can learn* to remain calm and undisturbed no matter what happens. Paul learned how to do this and we can, too. When we are faced with a crisis situation, we can stay calm by

32

keeping our eyes on the Lord and knowing that He is in complete control. If we keep trusting Him and refuse to waver in our faith, He will cause everything to work out for the best. "...*godliness* accompanied with contentment — that contentment which is a sense of *inward* sufficiency — is *great and abundant gain*" (I Timothy 6:6, *AMP*).

If we can keep our eyes on the Lord and trust completely in Him instead of reacting emotionally to whatever crisis we face, we will be able to stay calm in the face of adversity. We'll be able to do this because we know that the Holy Spirit within us is more than sufficient to take care of whatever comes against us if we'll just do our best and then let go, trusting completely in Him.

We can't escape from pressure, but we *can* refuse to allow pressure to overcome us. Ideally, we shouldn't allow ourselves to become worked up emotionally because of the problems that come upon us. They are all part of God's plan. "...*no man should be moved* by these afflictions: for yourselves *know* that we are appointed thereunto" (I Thessalonians 3:3, *KJV*).

If we react properly to pressure, the Lord will carry the load for us when we can't carry it any longer. When crises come up, if we have prepared ourselves by spending many long hours studying and meditating in our Father's Word, we will not panic. If our hearts are full of God's Word, we'll be able to bring up the appropriate verses of Scripture that have been stored deep down inside of us and act with unwavering faith on the promises and instructions that our Father has given us. This releases His power in our behalf.

People who spend all or most of their time in the world will turn to the *world* for help in troubled times. Christians who spend large amounts of time studying and meditating in God's Word *will turn to it.* There is no better foundation. "...God's truth stands *firm* like a great rock, and *nothing* can shake it. It is a *foundation stone...*" (II Timothy 2:19, *TLB).*

We need to build that solid foundation one brick at a time — one day at a time — with day after day of continued study and meditation in God's Word. When we react to adversity based upon God's Word, this puts *spiritual steel* into our lives. *We will not crumble.*

Our Father wants to use the problems in our lives to cause us to conform more and more to the image of Jesus Christ. We will do this if we react to these problems the way His Word tells us to react. When a crisis comes up, our hearts should be *so full* of God's Word that we *don't even have* to think what to do. We should react *automatically,* based upon the abundance of God's Word in our hearts.

God is a rock. He cannot be moved. If we truly do trust in Him, why would we ever allow anything to upset us??? We should never budge one inch from our rock-solid faith in Him. *"He alone is my rock and my salvation; he is my fortress, I will not be shaken"* (Psalm 62:6, *NIV).*

When the big problems of life hit us, we'll find out exactly how real God's promises are to us. Will we buckle under the strain? Or, will our faith in Him prevail? The answer will be determined by what we really believe deep down in our hearts.

Most Christians would agree that we should be like Jesus. He never changes. He doesn't react to external circumstances. He is always calm and confident, no matter what is happening. He lives inside of us. Instead of going through emotional ups and downs caused by reaction to external events, we should focus continually on the all-conquering, totally victorious Jesus Christ living in our hearts.

One of Satan's most effective techniques is to try to keep us worked up by *a succession of minor problems*. The cumulative effect of nagging, everyday, minor irritations often pulls us under. "...the little foxes, that spoil the vines..." (Song of Solomon 2:15, *KJV*).

We shouldn't fall into the trap of allowing the cumulative effect of the day-to-day, irritating problems of life to pull us under. This is why we need to get into our Father's Word each day. This is why we need to continually yield to and trust in Jesus Christ living inside of us. We need to keep ourselves spiritually strong so that the cumulative effect of the little problems of life will not be able to pull us down.

We are like marble. Our problems are like a sculptor. Our reaction to them determines how we will be shaped. They can be a horrible ordeal or a tremendous experience depending upon how we react to them. The greatest duty of adversity is to teach us that blessings are contained in the center of our problems if we'll just react to them the way that God's Word says to react.

God's Word is full of promises. In the period of time between learning His promises and receiving the manifestation of these promises we will always find one thing — a problem. *Our reaction to problems often determines the length and severity of these problems*. If we react in exact accordance to the instructions that our Father has given us, our problems often will be much less severe and will not last as long.

Our Creator didn't create us to be at the mercy of our emotions. He created our emotions to work *for us, not against us*. He has given us everything we need —the Word of God and the Spirit of God — to control our emotions instead of allowing them to control us.

Satan wants us to depend on our emotions, but

nowhere in God's Word are we told to depend upon our emotions. They often are unreliable. People who base their lives primarily on emotional response are headed for trouble. Our Father wants His children to live based on *faith* in His Word, *not* on our *feelings*. "...The man in right standing with God (the just, the righteous) *shall live by and out of faith*..." (Galatians 3:11, *AMP*).

People who habitually respond to their emotions are at the mercy of their feelings. Whatever can go way up also can go way down. Satan loves to see this roller coaster of emotions. God doesn't. He wants us to get on top of our problems and stay there. Jesus Christ has won a total, complete victory. He has given us the ability to rise above the trials and tribulations of this world.

We must not allow "the tail to wag the dog." Too many of us go from the valley to the mountaintop and back again. Too many of us reside at least semi-permanently in the valleys of life. This is not God's will. He wants us to rise above the problems in our lives and stay there.

His Word tells us exactly how to do this. If we spend too much time in emotional valleys, this is a clear indication that we either haven't paid the price to learn our Father's instructions or we don't believe deeply enough in them to follow them. If we learn to react the way that God's Word tells us to react, we'll always stay on top of the problems in our lives. "...*you* shall be *above only*, and you *shall not be beneath*, if you *heed* the commandments of the Lord your God, which I command you this day, and are watchful to *do them*" (Deuteronomy 28:13, *AMP*).

When we allow ourselves to be worried and afraid, we go through all kinds of ups and downs. However, if our hearts are filled with God's Word, they will sing with joy and we'll always stay on top of the problems in our lives, no matter what circumstances might come upon us. "...*he who has a glad heart has a continual feast [regardless of circumstances]*" (Proverbs 15:15, *AMP*).

Christians should not be *victims* of circumstance. Jesus Christ has given us *victory* over circumstance! We decide whether our reaction to the circumstances in our lives will end in "im" or "ory" — "victim" or "victory." If we truly believe in our hearts that Jesus has given us total victory in every area and acknowledge this in all our thoughts, words and actions, His victory will be manifested in every area of our lives. No matter what happens to us, we will not be defeated.

When the going is tough, we show by our words and actions which is predominant — the Word inside of us or the world outside of us. This is why it is so important to keep studying and meditating on God's Word — so that it will remain dominant over every circumstance that comes upon us. "...If ye *continue* in my word, then are ye my *disciples* indeed; and ye shall *know* the truth and the truth shall *make you free*" (John 8:31-32, *KJV*).

Our Father never intended for us to be controlled by emotional responses to adversity. When He created us, He created us in His image and gave us dominion over *all* things. Adam *gave up* this dominion. Jesus *won it back*. No matter what we are faced with, we can overcome it through Him.

The Lord knows everything that is happening to every one of us. "The eyes of the Lord are in every place, beholding the evil and the good" (Proverbs 15:3, *KJV*). When our faith is steadfast in Him, nothing will bother us because nothing bothers Him. No matter what the problem is, He can handle it.

When we focus continually on Jesus Christ living inside of us, we will be able to stand tall on the inside no matter what is happening on the outside. External problems shouldn't cause us trouble. Our troubles bother us to the degree that we allow these external problems to get *inside* of us.

We need to learn to take our eyes off the storms of life and keep them on the Lord. He will bring us through if we react with persevering faith. He rises above the storms. "...The Lord *has His way* in the whirlwind and in the storm, and the clouds are *the dust of His feet*" (Nahum 1:3, *AMP*).

Our Father's promises don't change in the midst of life's storms. They are always the same just as He is always the same. He doesn't waver and He doesn't want us to waver. Our reaction to problems should always be the same — to trust completely in Him. We'll always emerge victorious if we know His promises and refuse to waver one bit in our faith no matter how strong a particular storm might seem to be.

Chapter 5
Nothing Is Impossible For God

Webster's New World Dictionary says that the word "impossible" means "not capable of being, being done or happening." I don't know if there are dictionaries in heaven, but if so, we can be sure they don't contain this word.

Sometimes we run into problems that seem to be absolutely impossible...*for us*. Nothing is impossible for God. "...*With men* this is impossible; but with God *all* things are possible" (Matthew 19:26, *KJV*). We should never limit God in any way. "...with God *nothing* is ever impossible..." (Luke 1:37, *AMP*).

God created heaven and earth and He certainly can find a solution to any problem that exists in the midst of what He has created. Jeremiah said, "...Sovereign Lord, you have made the heavens and the earth by your great power and outstretched arm. *Nothing* is too hard for you" (Jeremiah 32:17, *NIV*). God agreed with Jeremiah. "I am the Lord, the God of all mankind. Is *anything* too hard for me?" (Jeremiah 32:27, *NIV*).

When everything seems to be falling apart, we can turn to the Creator of the entire universe for the help that we need. "My help comes from the Lord, the Maker of heaven and earth" (Psalm 121:2, *NIV*). If He could create the sun, the moon, the stars and all of the planets and keep all of them moving continually on their specific course, isn't it obvious that He can solve whatever problems any of us might have???

Jesus Christ was born of a virgin — that *seems impossible*, but it *happened*. Jesus rose from the dead

— that *seems impossible*, but it happened. Too many of us sell God short and give up way too soon.

In the spiritual realm, nothing is impossible. It might seem that way to our limited human understanding, but, fortunately for us, God's ways are much, much higher. He can instantly see thousands of ways to solve problems when our limited vision can't even see *one*.

God has ways to help us that transcend human understanding. When everything looks hopeless and we can't begin to see a light at the end of the tunnel, He already has the answer. There are no dead ends for our heavenly Father. He is the Master of every circumstance.

Too many of us allow problems to seem much bigger than they really are and God to seem much smaller than He really is. Nothing that will ever come against us will even *come close* to being as powerful as God is. If we add together all of the problems that we have had in the past, all of the problems that we face in the present and all of the problems that we could have in the future, the total of all of these problems won't even come close to being difficult for God.

Nothing is impossible for God. If anything is impossible, then He isn't Almighty God, is He??? No mountain is too high for Him to climb. No obstacle is too difficult for Him to go through, over or around. When we can't see the way, He can. He'll show us the way and He'll put a light on our paths. When the road is crooked, He will straighten it. He is with us always. He will never leave us. "I will *lead the blind by ways they have not known*, along unfamiliar paths I will guide them; I will turn the *darkness into light* before them and make the *rough places smooth*. These are the things I will do; I will *not* forsake them" (Isaiah 42:16), *NIV*).

No matter how great we think God is, He is much greater. No matter what we ask Him, He can do more. He can do much, much more than we think He can. He "*...is able to do exceeding abundantly above all that we ask or think, according to the power that worketh in us*" (Ephesians 3:20, *KJV*).

Just think about the words "exceeding" and "abundant." Exceeding means to *surpass* any limits that we might see. Abundant means *plentiful*, more than enough. There is absolutely *no limit* to what our Lord can and will do if we'll just trust in Him with strong, unwavering faith.

Yes, we will have problems, but no matter what problems we face, Jesus has already won a *victory* over them. "...In the world you have tribulation and trials and distress and frustration; but be of good cheer—take courage, be confident, certain, undaunted —for *I have overcome the world.—I have deprived it of power to harm, have conquered it [for you]*" (John 16:33, *AMP*).

We need to get our attention off the powerless problems that face us and focus our attention on the Powerful One and keep it there. No matter what we are faced with, we can handle it easily through the Victorious One who lives in our hearts. No problem is greater than the Lord Jesus Christ. No problem can stand up against His might and power.

All things are possible if we believe they are. "...*If* thou canst believe, *all* things are possible to him that believeth" (Mark 9:23, *KJV*). When we can't see a way out, there is one. He will find this way if we really believe that the God Of The Impossible will bring us through.

Our part is to trust God completely. His part is to figure out how to solve the seemingly impossible problem. He will always do His part if we don't block Him by failing to do our part. Jesus told us that faith can solve every problem. "...I tell you the truth, *if* you have faith as small as a mustard seed, you *can* say to this mountain, 'Move from here to there' and it *will* move. *Nothing* will be impossible for you" (Matthew 17:20, *NIV*).

Often we need to ask ourselves, *"How big is my God???"* Many of us are faced with big problems, but no problem is bigger than Almighty God's ability to solve it. He is bigger than any "mountains" that any of us will ever face. Too many of us are looking at medium-sized hills and treating them as mountains that are bigger than the Creator of the universe. This is wrong!!!

Satan's evil spirits continually whisper into our ears, exaggerating our problems and making them seem worse than they really are. This causes a tendency to "make mountains out of molehills." Our Father does just the opposite. The problems that seem like mountains to us don't concern Him in the least. *We must not allow our minds and hearts to shrink Almighty God down to the size of man.* We must realize the magnificent power of Almighty God and not allow our minds and hearts to minimize His power in any way.

Man's impossibilities are God's opportunities. When we have done everything we can do with our limited human ability, then it's time to let go and let the One who does not know the meaning of the word "impossible" to take over.

He will overcome the seeming impossibilities if we will stay calm in the face of adversity, showing our trust in Him by our tranquility. He is always at peace. His power flows in us, to us and through us when our calm, quiet confidence gives Him the channel to release this power.

Many of us get all worked up when we face a crisis. We rush around full of worry and agitation. This is *not* God's way. When everything goes wrong He wants us to become *very quiet* — to be *very still* —because we trust completely in Him. "...*be still*, and *know* — recognize and understand — that I am God..." (Psalm 46:10, *AMP).*

We need to remain calm if we want to get into the flow of God's power. He doesn't want us to be agitated and confused. Instead, He wants us to trust in Him. "In thee, O Lord, do I put my *trust*: let me *never* be put to *confusion*" (Psalm 71:1, *KJV*). If we are in right standing with Him (living according to the instructions in His Word), we will be quiet and confident at all times. "...the effect of righteousness shall be *peace* [internal and external], and the result of righteousness, *quietness* and *confident trust for ever*" (Isaiah 32:17, *AMP).*

When we have done all that we can do, our Father wants us to calm down and let go, letting Him take it from there. When we're calm and quiet, this enables us to *tune in* to the Holy Spirit who is always calm and quiet. If we allow ourselves to get tense and worked up, we *block* the flow of His power.

We need to be *still* in order to hear God's voice. Satan's voice is easy to hear. The more tense we are, the better we hear him. God's voice is just the opposite — we hear it best when we are still, calm and trusting. He is the Cornerstone of our lives and we should trust calmly and quietly in Him. "...he who *believes* — trusts in, relies on and adheres to that Stone — will *not* be ashamed or give way or make haste [in sudden panic]" (Isaiah 28:16, *AMP).*

If we have done what we should have done, our hearts will be full of God's Word. Satan cannot overcome us if our hearts are filled with the Word of God. "...the Word of God is (always in your hearts) *abiding in you,* and you have been *victorious* over the wicked one" (I John 2:14, *AMP).*

When we get aggravated, agitated or rattled, we react in the worldly realm, not in the spiritual realm. Our Father has given us quietness deep down inside of ourselves. When we calmly place our faith in Him in the face of a crisis, nothing can get at us. "When *He gives quietness* [peace and security from oppression], *who then can condemn?...*" (Job 34:29, *AMP).*

When we stay calm, God's strength is released. "...Their strength is to *sit still*" (Isaiah 30:7, *KJV).* In the spiritual realm, strength is the result of quietness and confidence. "...in *quietness* and in (trusting) *confidence* shall be your *strength...*" (Isaiah 30:15, *AMP).*

Receiving the strength of the Lord is very much like swimming. When we relax and trust the water, it will hold us up. If we panic and thrash and splash, we go under. If we'll stay calm and trust in the Lord, He will hold us up just as the water will hold us up.

When we calmly and confidently focus on the Lord, the confidence inside of us will cause us to rejoice and relax because we know that we are safe. "I have set the Lord *continually* before me; because He is at my right hand, I shall *not* be moved. Therefore my heart is *glad,* and my glory [my inner self] *rejoices;* my body too shall *rest* and confidently dwell in *safety*" (Psalm 16:8-9, *AMP).*

When we go through difficult times, *learning* from God's Word and *obeying* its instructions, we will be able to *remain quiet* and *calm.* "Blessed — happy, fortunate [to be envied] — is the man whom You discipline and instruct, O Lord, and teach out of Your law; that You may give him power to *hold himself calm in the days of adversity...*" (Psalm 94:12-13, *AMP*).

Satan wants us to panic and come apart at the seams. God wants us to stay calm, realizing that He is in control. Jesus never panicked. He always stayed calm in the middle of a storm. He lives inside of us today. He is still calm. He wants us to relax and turn to Him. If we do this, we can do all things through His strength.

If we have built a solid foundation of trust in the Spirit of God and the Word of God living in our hearts, we won't panic when we're faced with a crisis. We'll "know that we know" that the Lord is in control and that He will bring us through if we'll just relax and trust in Him. If we truly believe that God is in complete control, we'll wait patiently for the answer that we know is coming in His good timing. "*Be still* before the Lord and *wait patiently* for him..." (Psalm 37:7, *NIV*).

Our lives will be much, much better if we learn to stop reacting to the seemingly impossible situations that we face and, instead, to react only to the Spirit of God and the Word of God living in our hearts.

Chapter 6
The Lord's Timing
Is Different From Ours

One of the biggest problems that many of us face during a period of adversity is the length of time that we find ourselves spending in the midst of severe problems. If we pray with strong faith and then weeks (and sometimes months and years) go by and the problem is still there, some of us become discouraged and give up.

Our Father *never told us* that He would answer all of our prayers *immediately*. His timing is *much different* from ours. Most of us are in a hurry, but God isn't. Eagerness for a quick response doesn't make it come any faster.

Many times God will reply quickly to a prayer of faith, but this isn't always the case. God knows exactly what He's doing. He's not being slow just because we think He is. "...with the Lord one day is as a thousand years, and a thousand years as one day. The Lord does *not* delay and be tardy or slow about what He promises, according to some people's conception of slowness..." (II Peter 3:8-9, *AMP*).

We need to trust *completely* in His timing. "...my words are of a kind which will be fulfilled *in the appointed and proper time*" (Luke 1:20, *AMP*). He has a specific timetable for everything. "There is a time for *everything*, and a season for *every* activity under heaven..." (Ecclesiastes 3:1, *NIV*). His timing is perfect. He's never slow. Sometimes it just seems that way because our sense of timing is so different.

Should we expect Almighty God to change His

perfect timing to fit in with our imperfect timing?? He doesn't expect us to understand His timing. "...*It is not for you to know* the times or the seasons, which the Father hath put in his own power" (Acts 1:7, *KJV*). He will do His part if we'll do ours. Our part is to trust totally in Him...and this trust *includes* trusting in His timing.

In the Old Testament, it was definitely prophesied that the Messiah would be born of a virgin (Isaiah 7:14) and that He would be born in the tiny town of Bethlehem (Micah 5:2). However, many, many years went by before this great event took place. Why did God wait until that specific time to fulfill these prophecies? We don't know the answer.

God knew exactly when He wanted to send His Son to earth. He also knew why He would wait an additional thirty years until Jesus was thirty years old before He started His three-year public ministry. Jesus was very much aware of His Father's precise timing. On one occasion, His enemies tried to arrest Him but they couldn't because the time was not right. "At this they tried to seize him, but no one laid a hand on him, *because his time had not yet come*" (John 7:30, *NIV*).

Shortly after that He was teaching in the temple in Jerusalem. He could have been arrested, but He wasn't because the time was not right. "He spoke these words while teaching in the temple area near the place where the offerings were put. Yet no one seized him, *because his time had not yet come*" (John 8:20, *NIV*).

We see another example of the Lord's timing in the sickness, death and resurrection of His beloved friend Lazarus. When Jesus heard that Lazarus was sick, it seemed logical that He would immediately rush to His friend's assistance. *He didn't.* "Jesus *loved* Martha and her sister and Lazarus. *Yet* when he heard that Lazarus was sick, *he stayed where he was two more days*" (John 11:5-6, *NIV*). When Jesus finally arrived, Lazarus was dead. "On his arrival, Jesus found that Lazarus had already been in the tomb for four days" (John 11:17, *NIV*).

Martha knew that Jesus could have healed her brother. Most people would be very angry about this situation. Martha wasn't. In spite of the delay by Jesus and the death of her brother, Martha kept her faith. "'Lord,' Martha said to Jesus, *'if* you had been here, my brother would *not* have died. *But I know that even now God will.give you whatever you ask*'" (John 11:21-22, *NIV*). *This* is the kind of faith that our Lord is looking for! If He doesn't respond the way that we expect Him or when we expect Him to, He wants to see that we still trust Him.

Martha (and Mary) wanted their brother healed. However, Jesus had other plans. He purposely arrived late because He wanted to raise Lazarus from the dead. This is exactly what happened. "...Jesus called in a loud voice, 'Lazarus, come out!' The dead man came out, his hands and feet wrapped with strips of linen, and a cloth around his face. Jesus said to them, 'Take off the grave clothes and let him go'" (John 11:43-44, *NIV*).

Jesus gave us another example of God's timing when the time came for His arrest, crucifixion, resurrection and ascension. When that time came, He knew it. "...Before the Passover Feast began, *Jesus knew (was fully aware) that the time had come* for Him to leave this world and return to the Father..." (John 13:1, *AMP*).

We must be willing to trust God's timing. Sometimes He makes us wait because He has lessons that He wants us to learn from our problems and He waits until these lessons are thoroughly learned before He gives us His answer. We think we know how much we can endure, but God knows we can endure much more. He often will let us go through problems that we didn't think we could go through so that we can learn from them.

Sometimes our Father delays His answer because He wants us to draw closer to Him and He knows that an immediate answer wouldn't cause this to happen. Sometimes He doesn't answer quickly because He wants us to realize how helpless we really are. If we could have solved the problem, we would have. Sometimes we need to realize that only Almighty God can give us the answer.

Our Father often delays His answer because He wants our faith to be tried and strengthened. If He answered right away our faith wouldn't get much of an opportunity to grow. *Delays prove how strong our faith really is.*

Our Father often delays answering our prayers because He wants us to enlarge our future capacity to receive answers from Him. When we *know* that we're helpless and still hang on past the point where most people would have given up and *then* receive our answer, this causes our faith to *grow tremendously.*

If God doesn't answer right away, we can rest assured that an immediate answer isn't necessary. He knows what He's doing and He is never late. He will answer at exactly the right time *if* we keep our faith. "...these things I plan *won't happen right away.* Slowly, steadily, surely, the time approaches when the vision will be fulfilled. If it seems slow, *do not despair*, for these things will *surely* come to pass. *Just be patient! They will not be overdue a single day!*" (Habakkuk 2:3, *TLB).*

Instead of asking, "Why don't I have the answer

yet?", we should open our mouths and say, "Father, I don't doubt you in any way. I know that I have prayed according to your will. I know that you heard me. First John 5:14 tells me that I have the answer. I believe that you will manifest this answer in your perfect timing and I thank you for this, in Jesus' precious Name."

We know that we shouldn't pick fruit before it is ripe. This same principle applies in the spiritual realm. If we go against God's timing and try to force a result before the fruit is ripe, we cause problems. We need to study and meditate continually in the Word of God. Then we need to release our faith in these promises and wait patiently for their manifestation. When we do this, God will give us fruit "in season." "...his delight is in the law of the Lord, and on his law he meditates day and night. He is like a tree planted by streams of water, *which yields its fruit in season* and whose leaf does not wither. Whatever he does prospers" (Psalm 1:2-3, *NIV*).

Problems last for a *season*. The Lord knows how long that season is and why it needs to be that long. If we wait patiently and faithfully, we'll often find that the seemingly delayed answer is much more beneficial than a prompt answer would have been. We shouldn't lose heart if we don't receive an answer when we think we should receive it. If we give up, *how do we know* that we didn't give up just one hour or one day before we would have received God's answer???

Our Father wants us to live one day at a time, forgetting the past, trusting Him to bring us through this day and not concerning ourselves with tomorrow until tomorrow gets here. *"Forget the former things; do not dwell on the past. See, I am doing a new thing! Now it springs up; do you not perceive it? I am making a way* in the desert and streams in the wasteland" (Isaiah 43:18-19, *NIV).*

If we'll get our eyes off the past and keep them on the Lord, He will do a fresh, new work in our lives. He will make a way when there doesn't seem to be a way. If we can get our attention off the past and keep it focused on Him, then we'll be able to see the new way that He is opening up for us.

There is only one thing that the Lord wants us to remember from the past and that is how He has guided us. "And you shall (earnestly) remember all the way which the Lord your God led you..." (Deuteronomy 8:2, *AMP).* If we recall how we trusted completely and patiently in the Lord in the past and He brought us through, it will help us to trust Him again this time. When one door closes, another door opens. We need to get our attention *off* the closed door *in order to see* the new one that God is opening for us.

Carrying the burdens of the past into the present is one of life's biggest mistakes. Our Father gives us each day as a brand new experience — a fresh opportunity for a new start. "For you shall *forget* your misery; you shall remember it as waters that pass away. And your life shall be clearer than the noonday, *and rise above it;* though there be darkness, it shall be as the morning. And you shall be *secure* and feel *confident* because *there is hope...*" (Job 11:16-18, *AMP).*

Once we have forgotten the past, our Father wants us to do the best we can one day at a time and then to let go and let Him take care of the rest of the day, plus all of the tomorrows that have not come yet. He has given us everything that we need to deal with the burdens of life — one day at a time. Too many of us want to see too far ahead. There is nothing wrong with *planning* for the future, but it is definitely wrong to *worry about* the future.

51

Our Father seldom shows us two steps at a time. He wants us to take the one that we see and then He will show us the next one. He wants us to live in day-tight compartments. He wants us to shut the door to the problems of yesterday, and He wants us to shut the door to the anticipated problems of tomorrow. He wants us to walk with Him one day at a time, one step at a time.

If all of the problems of a lifetime were ever gathered together, they would be much more than we could possibily handle. This is why our Father allows *seasons* of adversity to come at us, giving us everything we need to deal with them one day at a time. When we can't see very far ahead, we need to go *as far as we can see*. The future is God's domain, not ours. He knows exactly what is going to happen, when it is going to happen and how it is going to happen. "...All the days ordained for me were written in your book before one of them came to be" (Psalm 139:16, *NIV*).

We need to forget the past, walk closely with the Lord in the present and not worry in the slightest about the future. "...*don't be anxious about tomorrow. God will take care of your tomorrow too. Live one day at a time*" (Matthew 6:34, *TLB*). There is no reason to be afraid of the future. We may not know what the future holds, but we do know Who holds the future. He is completely dependable. He will never change. "Jesus Christ is the *same* yesterday and today and forever" (Hebrews 13:8, *NIV*).

Chapter 7
Waiting On The Lord

When we are faced with a problem, we shouldn't run away from it. Instead, we should wait on the Lord, trusting completely in Him. Waiting on the Lord means to relax in the face of severe problems, knowing that, in His way and His timing, He will exchange His strength for our weakness if we trust completely in Him.

Jesus didn't win victory over *some* of our problems. He won victory over *all* of them. "...in *all* these things we are *more* than conquerors through him that loved us" (Romans 8:37, *KJV*). We are not just conquerors through Jesus. We are *more* than conquerors.

The word "more" wasn't used accidentally. Our Father put it in His Word to demonstrate the tremendous authority that His children have in the spiritual realm. No matter how difficult our problems might be, Christians have victory over these problems in exact proportion to our faith in the Lord. "For *whatever* is born of God *overcomes the world*; and *this* is the victory that has overcome the world — *our faith*" (I John 5:4, *NASV*).

This verse of Scripture tells us that every Christian who has been born again spiritually has been given victory over the problems of this world. *How* do we experience this victory?? We experience it *by faith* — by knowing what God's Word says, trusting completely in it and by continually showing faith in our words and actions.

No matter how long our Father requires us to

wait, we should be right there waiting because we trust in Him. We should know the promises in His Word that we are standing on and we should trust them — totally, completely and absolutely. We can trust the Lord. He protects us continually. "Let the beloved of the Lord *rest secure in him,* for *he shields him all day long...*" (Deuteronomy 33:12, *NIV*).

We don't have to take care of everything by ourselves. A God who is able to raise the dead certainly can handle *any* problem that is too difficult for us. "...we should *not* trust in *ourselves,* but *in God who raises the dead...*" (II Corinthians 1:9, *NASV*). Our Father will do His part if we'll do our part. Our part is to trust Him. His part is to bring the answer into manifestation in exact proportion to our trust in Him. "*According to your faith be it unto you*" (Matthew 9:29, *KJV*).

In a world of instant coffee, fast foods, Polaroid cameras, microwave ovens and other "instant" conveniences, it's difficult for many people to stand fast and not move. Most of us have many years of conditioning to the world's way of doing things and this is why many Christians find it very hard to wait on the Lord.

When we're faced with adversity, the carnal part of us wants to *get* going, to do something, anything. Of course we need to do whatever we can with our limited human abilities, but when we have done that, we need to stop and calmly let the Lord take it from there.

He will do the work if we will do the waiting, trusting completely in Him while we wait. Unfortunately, too many of us try to do His job for Him. We try to "*make things happen.*" This is just the opposite of what His Word tells us to do. "'...*Not by might nor by power, but by My Spirit,*' says the Lord of hosts" (Zechariah 4:6, *NASV*). Our Father doesn't want us trying to solve all of our problems with human might and power. He wants us to do the best we can with the limited abilities we have and then to wait on the Holy Spirit to take it from there.

We cannot wait on the Lord unless we trust Him. Deep, solid, rocklike, unwavering faith is the key to waiting on the Lord. He is in complete control. There is nothing for us to be concerned about. We should show our faith in His omnipotence through our humble, childlike, calm trust.

He wants so much to help us. "...the Lord has comforted His people and *will have compassion upon His afflicted*" (Isaiah 49:13, *AMP*). However, receiving this comfort is *not* automatic. We need to do our part. Our part is to *wait expectantly* on the Lord. "*The Lord is good to those who hopefully and expectantly wait for Him...*" (Lamentations 3:25, *AMP*).

One of the greatest promises in the Bible offers tremendous benefits to those who wait on the Lord. "...The Everlasting God, the Lord, the Creator of the ends of the earth does *not* become weary or tired. His understanding is *inscrutable*. He *gives strength* to the weary, and to him who lacks might He *increases power*. Though youths grow weary and tired, and vigorous young men stumble badly, yet those who *wait for the Lord* will gain *new strength*; they will *mount up* with wings like eagles, they will *run* and *not* get tired, they will *walk* and *not* become weary" (Isaiah 40:28-31, *NASV*).

These verses of Scripture say a lot! We are told that God never gets tired and that His understanding is beyond our comprehension. Next, we are told that even when vigorous young people get tired, the Lord *will give strength and power to us when we are weary and tired*.

How do we get this great strength and power?? *We*

get it by waiting on the Lord. We receive this strength and energy by refusing to be budged by circumstances, by holding fast and trusting completely in the Lord. What will happen if we do this? God's Word says that those of us who wait on the Lord and refuse to give in will receive supernatural new strength. We are told that we will mount up with wings like eagles and that we will then be able to run and walk without getting tired.

If our faith is strong and persevering enough to keep waiting on the Lord no matter how long it takes, He will give us wings like eagles. What do eagles do when they run into a storm? *They fly right over the top of the storm.* Eagles are able to fly so high that they can fly beyond the range of the most powerful binoculars. When they see a storm coming, they are able to set their wings so that the winds of the storm lift them and carry them *above* it. While the storm is causing havoc below, eagles *soar above them*, completely out of their range.

Eagles can soar to great heights. They also have tremendous strength. They are able to fly for miles and miles into a strong wind without getting tired. If our faith is strong enough, we can be like eagles, able to fly above storms and to keep on going without tiring.

Isaiah 40:28-31 is fascinating as we delve into it. The availability of this strength is confirmed by another verse of Scripture. *"Wait on the Lord: be of good courage, and he shall strengthen thine heart: wait, I say, on the Lord"* (Psalm 27:14, *KJV*).

Any time we see an instruction repeated in one verse of Scripture we know that the Lord wants to emphasize it. Psalm 27:14 starts and ends with a strong admonition to *wait* on the Lord in order to receive His strength. Many of us fail to receive many of our Father's promises simply because we don't maintain our faith long enough. It's not easy to wait on the Lord, but the blessings are well worth the effort. Everyone who trusts in the Lord enough to keep waiting will be blessed. "...blessed are *all* they that *wait for him*" (Isaiah 30:18, *KJV*).

When we wait on the Lord, this puts Him to work on our behalf. "...God...works and shows Himself active *on behalf of him who* [earnestly] waits for Him" (Isaiah 64:4, *AMP*). If we try to do everything ourselves, we usually will mess things up. If we do our best and then allow the Lord to take it from there, He'll work things out the way they should be. Our Father looks for His children who have enough faith to wait patiently on Him, trusting completely in Him even though our problems seem to be impossible to solve.

You might think, "That's easy to say, but *how* do I hang on during a time of severe adversity while I'm waiting on the Lord?" The answer is that we should hang on, based upon our faith in specific promises that His Word gives to us while we're going through difficult times.

For instance, our Father has given us a specific promise telling us that we'll never have to go through any trial that is beyond our endurance and, if we hang on, He will show us how to escape. "...*no* temptation or trial has come to you that is *beyond human resistance* and that is not adjusted and adapted and belonging to human experience, and such as man *can bear*. But God *is faithful* [to His Word and to His compassionate nature], and He [*can be trusted*] not to let you be tempted and tried and assayed *beyond* your ability and strength of resistance and power to endure, but with the temptation He *will* [*always*] *also provide the way out* — the means of *escape* to a landing place —that you may be capable and strong and powerful patiently *to bear up under it*" (I Corinthians 10:13, *AMP*).

There are many wonderful promises in this long verse of Scripture! Our Father knows exactly how much we can take. He will never allow us to have to put up with more than we can bear — one day at a time. Bridges have load limits. Elevators have load limits. Trucks have load limits. Human beings have load limits, too.

We are all different. Some of us can put up with more pressure than others. Our Father knows each of us intimately and He has promised that we'll never have to carry a load that is more than we can carry. If we truly believe this, we'll never allow ourselves the luxury of thinking that our problems are more than we can bear.

We can be comforted in knowing that, when the load becomes too heavy, He will give us rest. "Come to Me, *all* you who *labor* and are *heavy-laden* and *over burdened*, and I *will* cause you to *rest — I will ease and relieve and refresh your souls*" (Matthew 11:28, *AMP*).

So, we have a promise that our Father will never allow us to put up with more than we can bear and we have another promise that tells us that, when the load is too heavy for us to carry, Jesus Christ will carry it for us. Our Father never promised us an easy life, but He *did* promise everything we need to get through the difficult times.

As I have pointed out, I Corinthians 10:13 also promises us a way out — a way of escape. This doesn't mean this is "automatic." Our Father said that He would provide the *means* of escape. An escape route is always there, but we have to find it. Unfortunately, too many of us focus too much on the problem instead of looking intently for the escape — the way out that our Father has provided.

Chapter 8
Focusing On God Instead Of Focusing On Our Problems

When we are faced with severe problems, friends sometimes offer well-meaning advice such as "Hang in there," "Time will cure anything," "It's all going to work out for the best," etc. Some people tell us that we should "grit our teeth and hang on." Others say, "When the going gets tough, the tough get going." All of these sayings *sound* good, but they *don't offer much substance* to someone who is going through extremely difficult times.

When the going is really tough, we need to focus on the One who knows exactly what we're going through. He has great sympathy for us and He knows exactly what we need to do. Worldly solutions offer no relief. We need to draw close to the Lord who does offer the relief that we need.

He is all-powerful and in complete control of the entire universe. "...*the Lord our God the Omnipotent — the All-Ruler — reigns!*" (Revelation 19:6, *AMP*). No problem is bigger than He is. No matter *how big* our problems might be, they are *very small* compared to the magnificent power of Almighty God.

It is very easy to fall into the trap of overestimating the power of our problems and underestimating the power of our heavenly Father. This is not unusual. However, the truth is that there isn't anything that He can't handle. "I know that You can do *all* things and that *no* thought or purpose of Yours can be restrained or thwarted" (Job 42:2, *AMP*).

When we're going through difficult times, many of us tend to focus on our inadequacies. We know that we can't solve the problem. So what?? All of us are going to come up against many problems in our lives that are more than we can handle with our limited human ability. This is *no* reason to panic.

Our Father *never intended* for us to solve all of our problems with our human ability. When we can't go any further, He wants us to get our attention *off* the problem and *focus entirely on Him, trusting completely in Him.* He is in complete control, and His power is available to *every* one of His children who learns how to appropriate it.

Instead of focusing on problems, we should focus on the Lord Jesus Christ who has *all* of the power that any of us will ever need (and then some). "...*All* authority — *all* power of rule — in heaven and on earth has been given to Me" (Matthew 28:18, *AMP).* If we *really* believe this, *why* would we *ever* worry about *any* problem???? No matter how big a problem might *seem* to be, He is greater than *anything* that will ever come against us.

We trust pilots who we don't know to fly us from one place to another. We trust bus drivers, taxi drivers, elevators and bridges. *Why* should there be *any* hesitation to trust completely in the One who created us and loves us far more than we can possibly comprehend??

When we're in the midst of severe problems, we shouldn't back off one bit. Our Father has provided us with "...a kingdom that is firm and stable and cannot be shaken..." (Hebrews 12:28, *AMP).* We must not identify more with the problems of the world than we do with the immovable, unshakeable kingdom of God within us.

We need to take our eyes off the financial problem, the marriage problem, the health problem and all other problems and, instead, keep our attention focused on the Lord. This doesn't mean that we should absolutely ignore all problems. We ought to identify and acknowledge the problems that we are faced with, *but we shouldn't dwell on them.*

The eleventh chapter of Hebrews gives several examples of men and women who maintained their faith in God in the midst of very trying circumstances. We are told of Moses who "...never flinched but held staunchly to his purpose and endured steadfastly as one who gazed on Him Who is invisible" (Hebrews 11:27, *AMP*).

This is the attitude that our Father wants us to have. He wants us to get our attention off the visible and keep it on Him Who is invisible. When we're in a very dark situation, we should look for the light at the end of the tunnel and keep our eyes on it. God is light. Satan is darkness. We must turn towards the light. "...Let him who walks in the dark, who has no light, trust in the name of the Lord and rely on his God" (Isaiah 50:10, *NIV*).

It's so easy to blow our problems out of proportion to the point where they seem to be much worse than they really are. God doesn't want us to do this. He wants us to focus continually on Him. "I have set the Lord *always* before me. Because he is at my right hand, *I will not be shaken*. Therefore my heart is *glad* and my tongue *rejoices*; my body also will *rest secure*..." (Psalm 16:8-9, *NIV*).

When we take our eyes off the Lord and focus on "our" problems, this opens the door to Satan. However, when we take our eyes off the problems and look continually to the Creator of heaven and earth, this opens the door for Him to help us. "I will lift up mine eyes unto the hills, from whence cometh my help. My help cometh from the Lord, which made heaven and earth" (Psalm 121:1-2, *KJV*).

When we're in the midst of serious problems, God's Word tells us exactly what to do. "Let us *fix our eyes on Jesus*, the author and perfector of our faith, who for the joy set before him endured the cross, scorning its shame, and sat down at the right hand of the throne of God. Consider him who endured such opposition from sinful men, so that you will not grow weary and lose heart" (Hebrews 12:2-3, *NIV*).

God's Word tells us that we should fix our eyes on Jesus because He is our source. When we turn our eyes away from ourselves and fix them on Him, and keep them fixed on Him, we'll find the encouragement that we need when we're going through our "seasons" of difficult times. That's when our faith is tested. When our faith is being tested, we should focus on the One who is "the author and perfector of our faith." When we need strong faith, we should focus continually on the One who is the source of all faith. *His* strength will pull us through, not ours.

Jesus is the answer to every problem. Most Christians will mentally agree with this statement, but when we're under severe pressure, our words and actions often show that we don't really believe this in our hearts. Sometimes we don't turn immediately towards Jesus, trusting completely in Him. I know. I have done this.

Jesus should be our first resort, not the last. He is our solid Rock. He will protect us. He will deliver us if we'll keep our faith in Him. "The Lord is *my rock*, and *my fortress*, and *my deliverer*..." (Psalm 18:2, *KJV*).

When we're in a very difficult situation, all kinds of thoughts can come into our minds. Our Father wants us to throw out *every* thought that is contrary to His Word and to bring *every* thought into captivity to Jesus Christ. *"Casting down imaginations, and every high thing that exalteth itself against the knowledge of God, and bringing into captivity every thought to the obedience of Christ"* (II Corinthians 10:5, *KJV).*

The Greek word that is translated "imagination" actually means "reasoning." This verse of Scripture actually tells us to cast down seemingly logical human reasoning and the thoughts that Satan's evil spirits try to put into our minds. Instead, we are told to bring every thought into obedience to Christ — to think the way that God's Word tells us to think.

Our Father wants us to empty our minds of problems and worldly methods of attempting to solve problems. He wants us to fill our minds and hearts with His Word. This is where the answers are! Satan hates to see our minds and hearts filled with God's Word because this doesn't leave him any place to get in. God loves to see us thinking the way His Word tells us to think.

In fact, He has given us very specific instructions about the kind of thoughts He wants in our minds. "...whatever is true, whatever is noble, whatever is right, whatever is pure, whatever is lovely, whatever is admirable — if anything is excellent or praiseworthy — *think about such things.* Whatever you have learned or received or heard from me, or seen in me — *put it into practice.* And the God of peace *will* be with you" (Philippians 4:8-9, *NIV).*

Look at these words - "true," "noble," "right," "pure," "lovely," "admirable," "excellent" and "praiseworthy." *They describe Jesus Christ.* He lives inside of us in the form of the Holy Spirit. Instead of focusing on the problems in our lives, we should focus continually on the indwelling Christ — and all that we know about Him. We should yield our lives completely to Him, trusting completely in Him.

Our heavenly Father doesn't want us allowing the thoughts that evil spirits try to put into our minds to get a foothold. He wants us to *cast them out*. The word "cast" can be visualized by thinking of someone "casting" a fishing line. Just like a fisherman, we should *"throw"* these thoughts out — *as far away as we can cast them!*

God's Word *never* teaches us to focus our thoughts on the *problem*. It *always* teaches us to focus our thoughts on the *solution*. This is much easier to say than it is to do. Many of us have been so problem-centered for so many years that it isn't easy to make the change to always being God-centered.

There is only *one* way to do this and that is to diligently stick to a *daily* program of study and meditation in God's Word, continually learning what it says, turning it over and over in our minds and then meditating on it until it drops down into our hearts and comes from the abundance of our hearts up to and out of our mouths.

As this process continues for month after month, our trust in the Lord will grow steadily. When this trust is strong enough, it will enable us to keep our thoughts under control. Our hearts will be full of God's Word and it will be much easier for us to think the thoughts that our Father wants us to think and to cast out the thoughts that He doesn't want us to think.

The renewed mind focuses on solutions. The unrenewed mind focuses on problems. When we're under intense pressure, our minds *must* be renewed. Only a strongly renewed mind is able to turn away from extreme pressure and focus continually on Almighty God.

If we don't have a close daily relationship with the Lord, we're not suddenly going to be able to turn away from seemingly impossible situations and focus all of our attention on Him. There is *only one way* to keep our thoughts under control and that is to continually *commit* each day of our lives to the Lord. *"Commit* thy works unto the Lord, *and thy thoughts shall be established"* (Proverbs 16:3, *KJV).*

Instead of focusing on the problem, we need to focus continually on the promises that our Father has given us — promises that enable us to be part of His divine nature. "...He has granted to us His precious and magnificent promises, in order that *by them you might become partakers of the divine nature..."* (II Peter 1:4, *NASV).*

When we focus continually on problems, we partake of the nature of Satan. When we focus continually on the magnificent promises of God, we partake of His divine nature. Our problems are so very real. They are right in front of us. God's promises seem very distant to the unrenewed mind. They seem to be nice-sounding words, but not anywhere near as real as the severe problems that are pressing on us.

If we attempt to trust the Bible in the face of adversity, evil spirits whisper in our ears, "This is ridiculous. What can words from a book do against a problem as big as this one?" It's very difficult for a logical, reasoning, unrenewed carnal mind to believe that words from "a book" can be more powerful than a mind-boggling problem. However, the Bible isn't just "a book." It is God's Book — the Word of Almighty God.

We can't understand God's ways with our limited

human minds. This is why we have to continually study and meditate in His Word and confess it with our mouths in order to get it from our minds down into our hearts. This is where God's Word has to be in order to overcome our problems. "My son, *attend to my words; consent and submit to my sayings. Let* them *not* depart from your sight; *keep them in the center of your heart*" (Proverbs 4:20-21, *AMP*).

This is the key. We are told that God's Word should not depart from our sight. This means that we should study and meditate in it every day. This is how we keep His Word in the center of our hearts. When we study and meditate continually in God's Word, then we'll be able to submit to what it says and our faith in our Father's promises will be stronger than anything that comes against us.

There is no problem in the world that is greater than a believing heart trusting completely in the Word of God. Many of us lose out on receiving these precious promises because we haven't paid the price of building our faith to the point where we can rely totally on God's Word. "...the message they heard *did not benefit them, because it was not mixed with faith* [that is, with *the leaning of the entire personality on God in absolute trust and confidence in His power, wisdom and goodness*] by those who heard it..." (Hebrews 4:2, *AMP*).

We need to be very careful that we don't miss out on the precious promises that have been given to us. "...take care lest there be in any one of you a wicked, unbelieving heart — which refuses to cleave to, trust in and rely on Him — leading you to turn away and desert or stand aloof from the living God" (Hebrews 3:12, *AMP*).

We can trust completely in God's Word. "...He Who promised is *reliable* (sure) and *faithful* to His word"

(Hebrews 10:23, *AMP*). God is watching us to see if we will truly step out in faith so that He can do exactly what He says He will do. "...I am alert and active, watching over My word to *perform* it" (Jeremiah 1:12, *AMP*).

God sent His Word to deliver us from situations that would otherwise destroy us. "He sent his word, and healed them, and *delivered them* from their destructions" (Psalm 107:20, *KJV*). Our Father tells us exactly what He will do. Yet, in spite of this, many of us don't trust completely in what He tells us. "Yet in spite of this word you did *not* believe [trust, rely on and remain steadfast to] the Lord your God..." (Deuteronomy 1:32, *AMP*).

Our Father has given us *everything* that we need to take our minds off our problems and keep them on His promises. *If* we'll do what He tells us to do, our faith in His promises will *always* win out over our problems, no matter how severe they might be.

Chapter 9
Steadfast Endurance

As we go through the difficult problems of life, a great deal of patience and endurance is required. The Greek word *hupumone* that is translated as "patience" in the New Testament doesn't mean the same as "patience" means to us today — to "tolerate and put up with." What we call patience today is called "long-suffering" in the Bible. The word that is translated "patience" in the New Testament probably should have been translated "endurance," which means "the ability to last, to continue, to withstand pain, stress and fatigue — a calm, uncomplaining, unwavering, persevering quality that will not give up under severe pressure." In this chapter, the words "patience" and "endurance" will be used interchangeably.

Jesus said, "In your *patience* possess ye your souls" (Luke 21:19, *KJV*). Our souls are made up of our minds, our emotions and our ability to choose. When we're under pressure, all of us would *like* to be able to control our thoughts and emotions and be able to make the right decisions. *How* can we do this?? Jesus said that we do this by developing endurance.

Endurance is very pleasing to our heavenly Father. "...if when you do what is right and suffer for it you patiently endure it, this finds favor with God" (I Peter 2:20, *NASV*). If we hang on in the face of a seemingly impossible situation and refuse to waver in our trust in God, He will bless us with favor and turn seeming disaster into triumph.

If we *really believe* that our heavenly Father will do exactly what His Word says He will do, *why would we ever give up*??? When the going is tough, our Father wants us to learn to endure. "*...endure hardness*, as a good soldier of Jesus Christ" (II Timothy 2:3, *KJV*).

When it doesn't seem as though we can go one step further, our Father wants us to stand firm and unwavering. We don't do this in our own strength. We do this based on our faith in Him. Too many Christians give up. This denies the victory of Jesus Christ. He *will* bring us through if we *refuse* to waver in our faith. If we believe deeply in the promises in God's Word, we will not back down. We'll be spiritual "bulldogs." *Nothing* will be able to shake our belief that our Father will do exactly what His Word says He will do.

Our heavenly Father wants all of His children to develop great endurance. *How* do we do this? His Word gives us the answer. "...pressure and affliction and hardship produce patient and unswerving endurance" (Romans 5:3, *AMP*). If we pray to God for more endurance, He is very likely to respond by allowing us to go through pressure, affliction and hardship.

Am I saying that *everyone* who goes through pressure, affliction and hardship will develop strong, unwavering endurance? *No*! Many people go through difficult times and *fail to react the way that God's Word says we should react*. As a result, they come out weaker, not stronger. If we give up and lose, *we have to start all over again*.

The only way to develop strong, unwavering endurance is to face adversity the way that God's Word tells us to face it. If we do this, we pass the test and, when the next test comes along, we have more strength and endurance to use against it.

There is only one way to develop endurance and that is by enduring. We can prepare ourselves to endure by continual study and meditation in God's Word, but we also must put what we have learned into practice. When we fill our hearts with God's Word and hang on, refusing to give up, our perseverance will produce fruit. "...these are the ones who have heard the word in an honest and good heart, *and hold it fast, and bear fruit with perseverance*" (Luke 8:15, *NASV*).

All of us have our breaking points, but if we willingly pay the price of daily renewal of our minds and live our lives more and more the way that God's Word tells us to, we'll be able to endure much more. We'll get to the point where we're just starting to release our faith at the point where many people have already given up!

God's Word gives us many examples of the endurance of Jesus Christ. His endurance lives inside of Spirit-filled Christians. When our human endurance runs out, His supernatural endurance is available to us if we do our very best and then let go and trust Him to take it from there.

When there doesn't seem to be any way out, we must not give up. We must maintain our faith. *This* is when victory comes. We see an example of this in the Bible when some men brought a paralyzed man to Jesus to be healed and couldn't get into the house where He was because of the crowds. God's Word tells us about their refusal to give up:

"...some men were bringing on a stretcher a man who was paralyzed, and they tried to carry him in and lay him before [Jesus]. But finding no way to bring him in, because of the crowd, they went up on the roof, and lowered him with his stretcher down through the tiles into the midst in front of Jesus. And when He saw [their confidence in Him, springing from] their faith, He said, Man, your sins are forgiven you!" (Luke 5:18-20, *AMP*).

Those men *would not be denied*. They didn't look at the crowd and say, "We'll never get in to see Him." If they couldn't get in through the door, they were determined to find another way and they did — through the roof. Jesus honored their persevering faith and He *will* honor our faith *if* we refuse to let anything stop us.

We see another Biblical example of faith and perseverance in the story of Noah. God told Noah to build an ark. He built an enormous ship based upon God's exact specifications. "Make it 450 feet long, 75 feet wide, and 45 feet high" (Genesis 6:15, *TLB*).

God told Noah why he was to build this ship. "'Look! I am going to cover the earth with a flood and destroy every living being — everything in which there is the breath of life. All will die. But I promise to keep you safe in the ship, with your wife and your sons and their wives. Bring a pair of every animal — a male and a female — into the boat with you, to keep them alive through the flood. Bring in a pair of each kind of bird and animal and reptile. Store away in the boat all the food that they and you will need.' And Noah did everything as God commanded him" (Genesis 6:17-22, *TLB*).

Let's put ourselves in Noah's position while all of this was going on. This wasn't any little project. All of the wood for this boat had to be cut down from trees. It took a long time to build this ark. Can you imagine what people said to Noah during all of this time?? Can you imagine how he must have been ridiculed? Did he give up after five years?? or ten?? or twenty?? or fifty?? Did he allow the ridicule of others to cause him to quit?? No. *He never quit.* He did exactly what God told Him to do.

We need this same kind of faith and perseverance in our lives. We need to do exactly what God's Word tells us to, believing with all our hearts, absolutely refusing to give up. This isn't easy. We're going to get knocked down a lot. There isn't anything wrong with going down, but there is a *lot* wrong with *staying* down. God wants us to get up and start again. "...*Get thee up*; wherefore liest thou thus upon thy face?" (Joshua 7:10, *KJV*).

Babies don't walk the first time they try. They fall down again and again, but they get back up and keep on trying. This is what our heavenly Father wants us to do. When we start to fall, He *is* there to help us. "When he falls, he shall *not* be hurled headlong; because the Lord is the One who holds his hand" (Psalm 37:24, *NASV*). Again and again, God's children should get back up. "...though a righteous man falls seven times, *he rises again*, but the wicked are brought down by calamity" (Proverbs 24:16, *NIV*).

When we get up after being knocked down, our Father will give us a fresh start. Many of His greatest blessings have been given to His children who refused to stay down. He wants us to rise in faith, trusting completely in Him with steadfast endurance.

Faith is very important, but faith by itself often is not sufficient. There is often a time lag between the release of our faith and the manifestation of God's answer. While we're waiting to receive the answer, we must be calm and patient. "...we hope for what is *still unseen by us*, we wait for it with *patience* and composure" (Romans 8:25, *AMP*).

Faith and patience go together. Doubt and impatience go together. On many occasions, both faith and patience are required. "...be not slothful, but followers

73

of them who through *faith and patience* inherit the promises" (Hebrews 6:12, *KJV*). The word "slothful" means lazy. There are no shortcuts. We must be willing to pay the price of maintaining our faith over a long period of time in order to receive the promises of God. "*...after he had patiently endured, he obtained the promise*" (Hebrews 6:15, *KJV*).

Our Father will give us a wonderful reward when we are believing Him for something that is in His will and add strong endurance to our unwavering faith in Him. "*...do not throw away your confidence*, which has a great reward. For *you have need of endurance*, so that when you have *done* the will of God, you may *receive* what was promised" (Hebrews 10:35-36, *NASV*).

Too many of us throw away our confidence. We don't hang on tenaciously, absolutely refusing to waver. God wants us to "hang in there." He isn't pleased if His children give up. "...'my righteous one will live by faith. And *if he shrinks back, I will not be pleased with him*'" (Hebrews 10:38, *NIV*).

Like any father, our heavenly Father wants very much to bless His children. However, if we haven't paid the price of learning what His Word says He'll do (lack of knowledge), or if we don't believe that He'll do what His Word says He will do (lack of faith), or if we can't trust His timing to respond to our faith (lack of endurance), we *block* Him from the blessings that He wants *so much* to give us *if* we obey His instructions.

Too many of us are waiting for our Father to do something He has *already done*. He has given us His promises. They are ours. Through faith and patience we *can* receive these promises. He has done His part — He has given us thousands of promises. Our part is to *find* these promises in His Word, *trust* totally in

74

them and hang on with *endurance* until they have been manifested.

We need to stretch our faith as far as we believe it can be stretched and then, through patient endurance, we need to stretch it some more. Many Christians, especially newer Christians, don't hang on long enough. Too many of us "give it a try" and if we don't get an answer in a relatively short time, we give up, saying, "This faith stuff doesn't work."

It does work!! However, we must be willing to pay the price of building a solid foundation for our faith and then, *on top of* this foundation, we must be willing to hang on past the point where many people call it quits. **Too many of us allow Satan to steal the victory that Jesus gave us because we give up too soon!**

Our Father isn't always going to honor strong faith with an *immediate* answer. Sometimes His answer is delayed for as long as He, in His wisdom, deems it necessary to endure. If He answered all of our prayers quickly, we wouldn't build up much endurance, would we??

We must combine the two. Our Father gave us His Word to tell us how to hang on through the encouragement of His promises and patient endurance. "...everything that was written in the past was written to teach us, so that through endurance and the encouragement of the Scriptures we might have hope" (Romans 15:4, *NIV*).

When there doesn't seem to be any way out, we need to hang on, trusting totally in the Lord. He won't let us down. "...they shall *not* be put to shame who wait for, look for, hope for and expect Me" (Isaiah 49:23, *AMP*). If we refuse to give up, we will reap the results of our patient, enduring faith in God's appointed time. *"And let us not lose heart and grow weary and faint in acting nobly and doing right, for in due time and at the appointed season we shall reap, if we do not loosen and relax our courage and faint"* (Galatians 6:9, *AMP*).

Our lives are like a race. Our Father has set up a specific "race course" for each of us. He wants us to find the course that He has set for us and then to run this course with patient endurance and a steady, persistent faith. *"...let us run with patient endurance and steady and active persistence the appointed course of the race that is set before us..."* (Hebrews 12:1, *AMP*).

We do this by keeping our eyes on Jesus, by never wavering in the least in our faith in Him. Life is a long race. It is a marathon, not a sprint. We need a lot of faith and a lot of endurance to arrive safely at the finish line of the course that has been charted for us.

Victory doesn't come to the fast runners who trust in their own strength. *"...the race is not to the swift, nor the battle to the strong..."* (Ecclesiastes 9:11, *KJV*). Victory comes to the ones who hang on tenaciously with persistent, enduring faith in the Lord.

He is at the finish line. We need to keep our eyes on Him throughout the race, knowing that He will bring us through each stage of the race if we'll trust in Him and keep hanging on, knowing that His victory is our victory.

Chapter 10
Rejoicing
In The Midst of Adversity

We have just seen that we need to have an enduring faith as we face life's problems. It is so beneficial for us to develop this endurance that God's Word actually tells us to find joy from going through problems. *"Consider it wholly joyful, my brethren, whenever you are enveloped in or encounter trials of any sort, or fall into various temptations. Be assured and understand that the trial and proving of your faith bring out endurance and steadfastness and patience. But let endurance and steadfastness and patience have full play and do a thorough work, so that you may be [people] perfectly and fully developed (with no defects), lacking in nothing"* (James 1:2-4, *AMP).*

God's Word doesn't say to "consider it wholly sadness" when we run into trials. This is what most people do. It *doesn't make sense* to the average person's way of thinking to "consider it wholly joyful" whenever we come up against trials, tribulations and temptations. However, this is *exactly* what God's Word says to do. As we have seen, God's ways are very different from the world's way of doing things.

The word "wholly" means "entirely." We shouldn't "count it *partially* joyful" when we're going through difficult times. God's Word tells us that we should respond to every bit of trouble that we're going through with *total, complete joy.* God's ways certainly are different from ours, aren't they???

Why are we told to respond with complete joy

when we go through trials? God's Word says that we are *"assured"* that endurance, steadfastness and patience will come out of these trials (if we respond to them the way that He instructs us to respond). We need to take our Father's Word and believe that the results of going through these trials will be *so* beneficial to us in the future that we will be ecstatic about the opportunity to develop these highly desirable qualities.

God's Word doesn't tell us to run away from problems. We are never told to look for the easy way out. This is the world's way. God's way is to look at our problems with cheerful joy knowing that, *if* we respond properly to them, we will have a glorious opportunity to grow spiritually and be much, much better off as a result.

No matter what happens to us, we should always rejoice in the Lord. God's Word doesn't tell us to rejoice in the Lord *sometimes*. We are told to rejoice in Him *always*. In fact, our Father wants so much to emphasize this that He repeats this admonition *twice* in the same verse of Scripture. *"Rejoice in the Lord always — delight, gladden yourselves in Him; again I say, Rejoice!"* (Philippians 4:4, *AMP*).

We shouldn't just "put up with" trials and tribulations. God's Word tells us that we should actually rejoice in the midst of these trials and tribulations. What do we rejoice in? Do we rejoice in the problems? No, we are told to rejoice in the Lord. We don't rejoice in the problem. We rejoice in the Lord's victory over the problem.

When we can't see the answer, we should *still* rejoice because we know that Jesus Christ does see the answer and that He *can* and *will* bring this answer into manifestation *unless we block Him through doubt and unbelief*. We shouldn't rejoice based upon what does or doesn't happen to us. We should rejoice because the Victorious One lives inside of us.

Sooner or later, all of us are going to face severe trials and tribulations. Jesus told us this, but He didn't stop there. Why should we be *cheerful* in the midst of trials and tribulations? We should be cheerful because we *know* that He has total victory over every problem that any of us will ever face. "...In the world you have tribulation and trials and distress and frustration; *but be of good cheer — take courage, be confident, certain, undaunted — for I have overcome the world. I have deprived it of power to harm, have conquered it [for you]*" John 16:33, *AMP).*

Do we really believe this??? Do we honestly believe that, no matter *what* problem we are faced with, Jesus Christ has *already overcome it???* Do we honestly believe that Jesus Christ has *taken away* any power that our problems have to harm us??? If we *really* believe this, why then would we ever react with *sadness??* Of course we would react *cheerfully*!! *Why* would we ever respond with *anything except* joy and cheerfulness if we *really knew* that the problem could not defeat us???

Yes, we have total and complete victory, but there is one "catch." *We have victory here in the world to the degree that we deeply believe that we have this victory.* Our Lord wants to give us victory over *every* problem, but many of us *block him through unbelief.*

God's Word gives us a good example of how unbelief can rob us of blessings that the Lord wants so much to give. We see this in the story of Jesus returning to visit His home town of Nazareth. He had been performing amazing healing miracles everywhere. Doesn't it make sense that He would really want to perform these miracles among the people He had lived with for so many years — the people whom He knew so well?

However, when He went back, *they doubted Him.*
To them He was still the local carpenter. As a result,
"...He did *not* do many works of power there, *because*
of their unbelief — their lack of faith..." (Matthew
13:58, *AMP)*. We must be very careful that this doesn't
happen to us. The key to victory over problems is
complete trust in the Lord Jesus Christ.

Jesus is everything that the Word of God says He is
— and much, much more. His abilities are far beyond
our limited human comprehension. He "...is able to
[carry out His purpose and] do *superabundantly, far*
over and above all that we [dare] ask or think —
infinitely beyond our highest prayers, desires,
thoughts, hopes or dreams..." (Ephesians 3:20, *AMP)*.

Joy doesn't always come from favorable circumstances in our lives. It always comes from a deep love
for Jesus Christ and from a deep faith in Jesus Christ
regardless of what circumstances we might be faced
with. If we really do have a deep love for the Lord
and if we really do trust completely in Him, we will
always rejoice. *"Though you have not seen him, you*
love him; and even though you do not see him now, you
believe in him and are filled with an inexpressible and
glorious joy..." (I Peter 1:8, *NIV)*.

We rejoice because we know that the King of kings
and Lord of lords is protecting us and defending us.
"...let *all* those who take refuge and put their trust in
You *rejoice*; let them *ever sing and shout for joy,*
because You make a *covering* over them and *defend*
them; let those also who love Your name be *joyful* in
You and be in *high spirits*" (Psalm 5:11, *AMP)*.

Notice that the Word of God says that we should
"ever" sing and shout for joy. "Ever" means *"always."*
No matter what happens to us, we should always sing
and rejoice because the Lord is making a covering
over us — He is placing Himself between us and the
problem in order to protect us from its harm.

Psalm 5:11 goes on to tell us that if we truly do love the Lord, we will be full of joy and in high spirits. Love and trust go together. We trust the Lord because we love Him. Love is the foundation of Christianity. It is the *key* to faith. "...*faith which worketh by love*" (Galatians 5:6, *KJV*). Our love for the Lord and our limited understanding of His glorious love for us can keep our faith strong no matter what comes against us.

The Spirit-filled life — the life that is filled with, trusts in and yields to the living Christ within us — is a life of inexpressible joy regardless of what is taking place in the world around us. No matter how difficult our problems might be, our close relationship with Him fills us with comfort and an abundance of joy. "...With *all* our tribulation and *in spite* of it, I am *filled with comfort,* I am *overflowing with joy*" (II Corinthians 7:4, *AMP*).

There is no real joy in our lives unless we are able to trust the Lord. The world's "happiness" is dependent upon "happenings" — upon how well things are going in people's lives. The joy of the Lord is dependent upon our love for, trust in and closeness to Him. As we rejoice in the face of adversity, this actually brings us into contact with the Lord. "*Thou meetest him that rejoiceth...*" (Isaiah 64:5, *KJV*). Isn't this a beautiful promise???

One of the best ways to develop this close, joyous relationship with the Lord is to study and meditate in His Word on a daily basis. God and His Word cannot be separated. He gave us specific instructions which, if followed, will fill us with joy.

Jesus explained this when He said, "...if you *continue to obey* My instructions — *you will abide in My love and live on in it*; just as I have obeyed My Father's commandments and live on in His love. I have told you these things that *My joy and delight may be in you,* and that your joy and gladness may be *full measure* and *complete* and *overflowing*" (John 15:10-11, *AMP*).

Isn't it interesting to see that love and joy are directly connected to knowing and obeying the instructions that have been given to us in the Word of God??? *This is why God's Word was written.* "And these things write we unto you, *that your joy may be full*" (I John 1:4, *KJV*).

When difficult times come upon us, we *can* continue in the joy of the Lord *if* our hearts are filled with His Word. God's Word is our *spiritual* food. When we study and meditate in it each day, this feeds us in the spiritual realm and causes us to rejoice deep down in our hearts. "Your words were found, and I ate them, and *Your word was to me a joy and the rejoicing of my heart...*" (Jeremiah 15:16, *AMP*).

Our Father does not lie. If His Word says He will do something, He *will* do it (unless we block Him through doubt and unbelief). "God is not a man, that he should lie, nor a son of man, that he should change his mind. Does he speak and then not act? Does he promise and not fulfill?" (Numbers 23:19, *NIV*). He does exactly what His Word says He will do. *If we will do our part* — study, meditate, trust and obey — *He will do His part.* "...I have spoken, and I *will* bring it to pass; I have purposed it, and I *will* do it" (Isaiah 46:11, *AMP*).

We should rejoice because we know that the Word of God is true. We also should rejoice because we know that the Lord is with us always — all day long, every day of our lives, no matter what is happening to us. He will never leave us. He will always help us. We shouldn't be afraid of anything.

It's so beautiful to know that the Lord of the

universe lives inside of us, that He is with us all day long, every day of our lives and that He will never leave us. Our hearts will just sing with joy when this great truth gets off the pages of His Word, into our minds and, from there, right down into the center of our hearts.

There is no joy that can even begin to compare to the joy that is ours when every hour of every day our lives are truly centered around, trusting in and yielded to the Holy Spirit living in our hearts. We already have the joy of the Lord living inside of us because the Holy Spirit lives inside of us.

Joy is a *fruit* of the Holy Spirit. When we *refuse* to allow our selfish desires, worldly circumstances or anything else to control our lives but, instead, cheerfully allow the Holy Spirit to *control* every aspect of our lives, His joy (and His other fruit) will be produced in our lives. "...when the Holy Spirit *controls* our lives he will produce this kind of fruit in us: love, *joy*, peace, patience, kindness, goodness, faithfulness, gentleness and self-control..." (Galatians 5:22, *TLB*).

When we trust completely in the Holy Spirit, we won't be worried or depressed because His joy will strengthen us. "...be *not* grieved and depressed, for *the joy of the Lord is your strength and stronghold*" (Nehemiah 8:10, *AMP*). In the spiritual realm, joy is the source of strength. The joy of the Lord strengthens us. When we rejoice in the midst of trials and tribulations, then we are able to do all things through the strength of the Lord.

When we're going through fiery trials, *this* is the time to glorify the Lord. "...*glorify ye the Lord in the fires*..." (Isaiah 24:15, *KJV*). When everything seems to be falling apart, God's Word actually tells us that we should laugh. "...neither shall you be afraid of destruction when it comes. At destruction and famine *you shall laugh...*" (Job 5:21-22, *AMP*).

This doesn't make sense to a logical, unrenewed, carnal mind. *Why* should we laugh when everything is going wrong? We should laugh and rejoice because we *know* that the Lord is completely in control. If we truly believe this deep in our hearts, then we will be able to rejoice and laugh no matter how difficult the problems might seem.

Our Lord is *much, much greater* than anything that will ever come against us. Circumstances are *never* greater than the Lord. *We must not allow the lesser to overcome the greater*. We *give up our joy* whenever we believe that the circumstances around us are greater than the Lord within us.

Chapter 11
How Do All Things Work Together For Good?

We have just seen how important it is for us to rejoice in the face of adversity. However, some of us do exactly the opposite. When the going is tough, some of us *complain*. Irritated, complaining Christians are not joyous Christians.

Our Father does *not* want His children to complain. "...When the people complained, it *displeased* the Lord..." (Numbers 11:1, *KJV*). Whether we realize it or not, when we complain about something, we're really complaining about God. If we really believe that God is in complete control of everything, then our complaints actually say, "God, I'm complaining because I don't like the fact that you let this happen."

Too many of us complain about the very circumstances that God has allowed to take place in order to teach us what He, in His infinite wisdom, knows that we need to learn. If we could only see the opportunities that God can see in the midst of problems, we would stop complaining.

Many times the very things that we are complaining about will work out for our good. One of the best-known verses of Scripture tells us, "And we *know* that God causes *all* things to *work together for good* to those who *love God*, to those who are *called* according to His purpose" (Romans 8:28, *NASV*). Many Christians don't even begin to understand what this says. There is much more depth to this magnificent verse of Scripture than most of us realize. Let's take it apart piece by piece to see what it *really* says.

The first key is the word "know." Romans 8:28 doesn't say that we "hope" that all things work together for good. It says that we *know* that all things work together for good. The word "know" means "to be certain, to be sure."

The next key word is "all." God's Word doesn't say that "some" things or "most" things work together for good. We have just read that "...God causes *all* things to work together for good..." Over the course of a lifetime, this word "all" includes tens of thousands of occurrences in our lives. We are told that God can cause every one of them to work towards our best interest.

The words "know" and "all" aren't debatable. They are very clear. Most people understand these two words. Where most people fail to understand Romans 8:28 starts with the word "together." Romans 8:28 does *not* say that every single thing that happens to us will work out just the way we want it to. It says that God can cause everything that happens in our lives *to combine together* to work out for our best interest. Our heavenly Father is able to mix all of the ingredients of our lives together — ingredients which may not seem to be good all by themselves — and cause them to produce an ultimate result that is very good.

Again, I want to emphasize that God's Word does *not* say that every single instance works out perfectly. If we tell this to someone who is hurting, we are giving them unscriptural advice. This is very obvious. Most of us know many Christians whose problems haven't worked out well at all.

The Amplified Bible's version of Romans 8:28 says, "...all things work together and are [*fitting into a plan*] for good..." The amplification of the original

Greek tells us that everything that happens to us actually *fits into a plan* that God has for our lives on the whole — not only here on this earth but also for eternity in heaven.

Now that we have taken a good look at the words "know," "all" and "together," we need to look further. The provisions of the first half of this verse of Scripture do *not* apply to everyone. We are told that we know that all things work together for good only for those who:

(1) *love God* and,

(2) *are called according to His purpose.*

These two conditions eliminate many people. Let's see what each of them really says. Let's start with loving God. I ask each reader to stop right here and think for a minute. What do you think it means to "love God"? *What is your definition of this?* Before reading any further, please *stop* and take time to come up with a precise definition. This is important.

Now, let's see what God's Word says about this. Jesus told us what it means to love Him. He said, "If anyone loves me, *he will obey my teaching...*" (John 14:23, *NIV*). We show our love for the Lord the *same way* that little children here on earth show love for their parents — by *obeying* the instructions that are given to them.

How can we obey His instructions if we don't know what they are??? The very *first* thing that we need to do in order to show our love for God is to *hunger* and *thirst* for His Word — to deeply desire to learn everything that we possibly can about how He wants us to live our lives.

If we really do love God, then we will want to live our lives the way that He wants us to live them. *How* do we do this? We are told that we win His approval by studying His Word. *"Study* to show thyself approved unto God..." (II Timothy 2:15, *KJV*).

God's ways are very different from what seems right to logical, worldly-oriented reasoning. *This* is why our love for God must *start* with continually studying and meditating in His Word. This wins His approval because loving God means *obeying* Him — finding out what His instructions are and then doing our very best to follow these instructions.

The final portion of Romans 8:28 tells us that this verse of Scripture applies "to those who are called according to His purpose." *What* does this mean? Our Father's purpose is *His will for us*. He has a plan for each of us. He has called each of us to a definite mission in life.

If we want all things to work together for good in our lives, we need to find what God has called us to do and to get into His will and stay there. "The God of our forefathers has destined and appointed you to come progressively to *know His will* — that is, to *perceive, to recognize* more strongly and clearly and *to become better and more intimately acquainted with His will*..." (Acts 22:14, *AMP*).

We should continually seek God's will. *Nothing* is more important. We have to get ourselves and our desires out of the way! Then our lives will give us much more meaning and fulfillment. "...learn to *put aside your own desires* so that you will become patient and godly, *gladly letting God have his way with you*" (II Peter 1:6, *TLB*).

No matter how much human ability and strength we might have, our Father doesn't want us doing things our way. We must seek His will continually, yielding each day of our lives to Him. "...the way of a man is *not* in himself. It is *not* in man [even in a strong man and a man at his best] to direct his own steps" (Jeremiah 10:23, *AMP*).

The desire to find God's will for our lives and to yield to the Holy Spirit within us should consume us. "...*be aglow and burning* with the Spirit,serving the Lord..." (Romans 12:11, *AMP*). Our Father's Word tells us that we should set our faces like flint to do His will. Flint is a very hard kind of rock. Our Father wants us to be rock-solid and unyielding in our determination to live our lives the way that He wants us to live them. If we do this, we will come out on top no matter how difficult our problems are. "...I have set my face like *flint* to *do his will*, and I *know* that I *will* triumph" (Isaiah 50:7, *TLB*).

If we get into our Father's will and stay there, He will provide everything we need. He will "equip you with *everything good* for doing his will..." (Hebrews 13:21, *NIV*). Our Father "...*works out everything* in agreement with the counsel and design of His [own] will" (Ephesians 1:11, *AMP*).

If we continually stay in our Father's will once we find it, we can stand firm in the face of all adversity, knowing that He will take care of everything for those who continually seek to stay in His will. "...my dear brothers, *stand firm*. Let *nothing* move you. Always give yourselves *fully* to the work of the Lord, because you *know* that your labor in the Lord is *not* in vain" (I Corinthians 15:58, *NIV*).

As we look more in depth at Romans 8:28, we can see clearly that this is a *conditional* promise. God's part is to guarantee us that *everything* that happens to us *will* work out for our good. He doesn't guarantee this for everyone. No, He offers this promise to those children who *love Him* (who learn and obey His instructions, trusting in Him with unwavering faith) and to those children who *do their very best* to live according to *His purpose* for their lives — to continually seek to find and stay in His will.

All of us need to evaluate ourselves honestly in relation to our part of Romans 8:28. *Do we* really love God — do we study and meditate continually in His Word to find His instructions and obey them?? *Do we* continually seek His will for our lives — to find the purpose that He has called us to and to stay in His will to the best of our ability month after month and year after year??

Our Father will always do His part if we will do our part. So many of us miss out because we're so short-sighted. We tend to focus primarily on this short life here on earth — especially right now — this day, this week, this month, this year. Our Father looks at our lives much differently.

He looks at eternity. He causes all things to work together for good not just here and now on this earth, but over the endless years of eternity. Many of the things that will ultimately work out for our eternal good can't even be comprehended by our limited human understanding. **Romans 8:28 is not limited to this life.** Many of the things that seem so bad in this life have eternal dimensions that we'll never begin to understand until we're in heaven. Then we will understand many things that are impossible to understand now.

Our Father is in complete control. Sometimes it doesn't look that way to our limited understanding, but we can rest assured that He is Almighty God and that He is in control. *If* we learn what His Word says and obey these instructions to the best of our ability, continually seeking to find and obey His will for our lives, trusting completely in Him, we can rest assured that He *will* cause *all* things to work together for our good.

If we really believe this, we won't complain. Complaining *closes* the door to God and opens the door to Satan. "...I complained, and *my spirit was over-whelmed...*" (Psalm 77:3, *KJV*). When we rejoice in the face of adversity, *just the opposite happens* — we *close* the door to Satan and *open* the door for our Father's blessings.

When we open our mouths and let complaints come out, we *deny* the victory that Jesus Christ won for us. We give spiritual power to a powerless Satan and his evil spirits and we *block* the power of the Holy Spirit and His legions of angels from being released on our behalf. If we do complain, we need to repent and ask our Father to forgive us.

As we learn to trust God completely because we are doing our part of Romans 8:28, we'll never complain and we'll always rejoice because we will know that He is doing *His* part of Romans 8:28.

Chapter 12
Giving Thanks To The Lord

Now that we have seen the importance of always rejoicing and never complaining, we should see exactly how to go about doing this. One way to do this is to continually thank the Lord.

Our Father's Word tells us that giving thanks is beneficial. "It is a *good thing* to give thanks unto the Lord..." (Psalm 92:1, *KJV).* No matter what we say and do, we should continually thank our heavenly Father through our Lord Jesus Christ. "...*whatever* you do, whether in word or deed, do it *all* in the name of the Lord Jesus, *giving thanks* to God the Father through him" (Colossians 3:17, *NIV).*

We should give thanks to the Lord whenever we go to church. "I will give thee thanks *in the great congregation*: I will praise thee *among much people*" (Psalm 35:18, *KJV).* We should sing our thanks to the Lord. "*Sing* unto the Lord with thanksgiving..." (Psalm 147:7, *KJV).*

If we wake up in the middle of the night, we should thank the Lord. "At midnight I rise to give you thanks for your righteous laws" (Psalm 119:62, *NIV).* There is never a time when we shouldn't be thanking the Lord. No matter what happens to us, our Father wants us to thank Him. "In *every thing* give thanks: for *this is the will of God* in Christ Jesus concerning you" (I Thessalonians 5:18, *KJV).*

Let's look closely at this verse of Scripture. Our Father's Word *doesn't* tell us to give thanks when "*some*" things happen to us. It says to give thanks in "*all*" things. No matter what happens to us, we are told to give thanks because it is God's will for us to do this.

This has created quite a bit of controversy among Christians. Many Christians say, "Why should I give thanks for what Satan does?" *Should we* give thanks if the doctor says that we have cancer?...if a family member is killed?...if our automobile is stolen?...if we lose our job?, etc., etc.?

Some Christians say that this is exactly what we should do and they point to the following verse of Scripture as an example: "Giving thanks always *for all things* unto God and the Father in the name of our Lord Jesus Christ..." (Ephesians 5:20, *KJV*).

Let's take a further look at this verse of Scripture which seems to tell us to give thanks "for" all things. I'm not a Greek scholar, but I don't believe that the word "for" is a correct translation. The Greek word ("haper") which is translated "for" is a preposition which also means "over," "above," "beyond." I believe we should always thank God because of the victory that we have *over*, *above* and *beyond* all negative things that happen to us.

I don't believe that we thank the Lord *for* our problems. Instead, we should thank God for the *victory* that the Lord Jesus Christ has given us over all problems. "...thanks be unto God which *always causeth us to triumph* in Christ..." (II Corinthians 2:14, *KJV*).

No matter what Satan tries to hit us with, *we have the victory*. Jesus told us that He has given us the authority to walk all over the serpent (Satan) and his scorpions (evil spirits). No matter what they try to do to us, they cannot defeat us if our faith is strong, enduring and unwavering. "...I give unto you power to *tread on serpents and scorpions*, and over *all* the

93

power of the enemy: and *nothing shall by any means hurt you"* (Luke 10:19, *KJV).*

Jesus Christ was sent to this earth to destroy the work of Satan. "...For this purpose the Son of God was manifested, that he might *destroy* the works of the devil" (I John 3:8, *KJV).* He *accomplished* this mission. This is why Jesus said,"...it is *finished..."* (John 19:30, KJV) as He hung on the cross at Calvary.

If Jesus has *all* power, *how much* power does that leave to Satan??? *Satan has no power except the power that we give him through lack of faith,* through believing that the problems that come against us are greater than Jesus Christ living inside of us.

We should *never* allow ourselves to think this. No matter what Satan tries to do to us, it is never more powerful than Jesus Christ living inside of us. No matter what comes against us, Jesus has won victory over it. If we *really* believe this deep down in our hearts, *then why wouldn't we give thanks in the midst of adversity???* If we know that we're going to win (if our faith endures and we absolutely refuse to waver) we won't hesitate to give thanks.

This victory isn't "automatic." It is *only* ours if our faith is *strong* and *enduring* and *refuses* to give in, no matter how difficult our problems might be. The faith that enables us to give thanks to the Lord no matter what happens to us comes *only* from deep-rooted conviction based upon many, many hours of filling our hearts with God's Word and drawing closer and closer to the Lord. "...as you trusted Christ to save you, *trust him, too, for each day's problems; live in vital union with him. Let your roots grow down into him and draw up nourishment from him.* See that you go on *growing* in the Lord, and become *strong* and *vigorous* in the truth you were taught. Let your lives *overflow* with joy and thanksgiving for all he has done" (Colossians 2:6-7, *TLB).*

When we are going through adversity, it is very important to meditate on these two verses of Scripture until they are deep down inside of our hearts. We are told that the *same faith* that we used to initially receive Jesus as Saviour *should also be used with the daily problems that we face.*

We should be close to the Lord at all times — in "vital union" with Him. We should work steadily at building our faith so that our spiritual roots will go down deep and enable us to draw our sustenance from the Lord. If we continually grow in the Lord, the truth of God's Word in our hearts will give us the faith that we need in order to rejoice and thank the Lord for the wonderful victory that He has given us.

When we're tempted to give in to worry and fear, we should give thanks instead. Jesus lives inside of us and He will help us if we'll just release our faith. A continual attitude of thanksgiving in the face of the problems shows our faith and creates the channel in the spiritual realm through which our Lord can bless us and deliver us from problems.

Too many of us fail to give thanks to God. Even though we know that He is Almighty God, many of us fail to give thanks to Him continually. "...when they knew and recognized Him as the God, they *did not* honor and glorify Him as God, *or give Him thanks...*" (Romans 1:21, *AMP*).

If we fail to give thanks continually, this often blocks us from receiving blessings. When we thank the Lord in the face of adversity, this opens the door for Him to bless us. "*Enter into his gates with thanksgiving...*" (Psalm 100:4, *KJV*). Continued, bold thanks in the face of adversity brings us right into the presence of Almighty God. "*Let us come before His presence* with thanksgiving..." (Psalm 95:2, *AMP*).

This is so beautiful!!! As gruesome as the prospect

is, just imagine for a minute that you are Satan and that you are trying your best to destroy a certain Christian, but this Christian refuses to bend. Instead, he keeps on thanking God for the victory that Jesus has given him. As this Christian keeps on thanking God, his continued attitude of thanksgiving *brings him right into the presence of God.* **What does Satan do when he is face to face with God? He runs away!!!** "Submit yourselves therefore to God. Resist the devil, and *he will flee from you*" (James 4:7, *KJV).*

We submit ourselves to God when we follow His instructions to continually give thanks no matter what is happening to us. When we do this continually in the face of severe adversity, *Satan cannot handle the pressure and he runs away,* looking for someone else with much less faith and endurance. "...Your enemy the devil prowls around *like* a roaring lion *looking for* someone to devour" (I Peter 5:8, *NIV).*

Many Christians don't understand what this verse of Scripture really says. It does *not* say that Satan is a roaring lion. It says that he is *like* a roaring lion. He looks like a roaring lion, but he isn't. Jesus Christ knocked his teeth out two thousand years ago. He is "all bark and no bite."

This is why God's Word says that he has to *"look for* someone to devour." If he really was a roaring lion, he could devour anyone, couldn't he?? Because he isn't a roaring lion, he has to *look for* someone who he can deceive—someone who doesn't fully realize the total, complete victory that we have in Jesus Christ. He has to *look for* someone who won't persevere in faith and keep on thanking the Lord no matter how difficult our problems might seem to be.

It isn't easy to thank God when the going is tough. This goes completely against our natural inclination which is to complain. We have to deny our natural instincts and sacrifice in order to thank God at such a difficult time. However, if we release our faith by continually thanking God even when we don't feel like it, He will deliver us out of our troubles. "Offer to God the *sacrifice* of thanksgiving; and pay your vows to the Most High, and call on Me in the day of trouble; *I will deliver you,* and you shall honor and glorify Me" (Psalm 50:14-15, AMP).

Isn't this beautiful?? Isn't it great to see how all of these pieces about giving thanks fit together? **The Lord is so good. He is so merciful. We have so much to thank Him for.** "O *give thanks* unto the Lord; for he is *good*: for his mercy *endureth forever*" (Psalm 136:1, KJV).

One final area where emphasis is placed on giving thanks is when we pray to God. When we pray, we should always give thanks. "Devote yourselves to prayer, keeping alert in it *with an attitude of thanksgiving*" (Colossians 4:2, NASV).

Why are we told to give thanks as we pray? The answer is that this shows our faith. **If we really believe that God is going to answer our prayer, what is more natural than to thank Him as we pray?** *We don't have to wait* until we see the answer before giving thanks. This isn't faith. Faith thanks God *before* the answer is manifested in the natural realm.

When we pray, we often come to God with a problem. Are we going to worry about that problem or are we going to *pray with faith?* If we show our faith as we pray by thanking God and by maintaining this faith while we are waiting for His answer, we will experience God's peace which is *so great* that we can't comprehend it with our limited human understanding. "*Don't worry about anything*; instead, pray about everything; *tell* God your needs and *don't forget*

97

to *thank him for his answers. If* you do this you will experience *God's peace,* which is *far* more wonderful than the human mind can understand. His peace will *keep* your thoughts and your hearts *quiet* and *at rest* as you trust in Christ Jesus" (Philippians 4:6-7, *TLB).*

Instead of giving thanks only when things go our way, God's Word clearly shows us again and again that we should react to problems in our lives by continually thanking Him. We should thank God continually because, no matter how bad the situation might seem to be, He *is fully capable* of turning everything that happens to us into a blessing. Our continued faith and attitude of thanksgiving provide Him with the channel that He is looking for in order to give us this blessing.

Chapter 13
Praising The Lord At All Times

In this chapter we're going to take a good look at a subject that is very similar to giving thanks, and that is praising the Lord. When we give thanks we thank the Lord for what He has done or for what we know by faith He is going to do. When we praise the Lord, we give Him praise for who He is.

God's Word instructs us to give thanks to Him continually. When we're in the midst of a severe problem, praise and thanksgiving are the keys to maintaining the joy of the Lord. "Let the joys of the godly *well up in praise* to the Lord, for *it is right* to praise him" (Psalm 33:1, *TLB)*.

It's easy to praise the Lord when the sun is shining, our health is good, we're getting along well with everyone, we have money in the bank and everything else is going well. *The real test comes when everything is going wrong.* Do our hearts *still* sing for joy?? Does praise *still* pour out of our mouths?? Is our praise *unaffected* by circumstances?

Our Father definitely wants us to praise Him. This is one of the reasons why He created us. "This people have I formed for myself; *they shall show forth my praise*" (Isaiah 43:21, *KJV)*. He is always pleased when we praise Him and He is especially pleased when we praise Him in the midst of trials and tribulation. He wants us to make this "sacrifice" at all times, not just when things are going well. "...Let us *constantly* and

at all times offer up to God a *sacrifice* of praise..."
(Hebrews 13:15, *AMP*).

Our Father told the Israelites that, if they would
offer this sacrifice, He would restore the fortunes of
their lands. This principle also applies to each of us
with our individual problems. "...Praise the Lord of
hosts: for the Lord is good; for his mercy endureth for
ever: and of them that shall bring the *sacrifice of
praise* into the house of the Lord. For I *will* cause to
return the captivity of the land, as at the first, saith
the Lord" (Jeremiah 33:11, *KJV*).

Our Father wants us to praise Him at all times. "I
will bless the Lord at *all* times: his praise shall
continually be in my mouth" (Psalm 34:1, *KJV*). We
should praise Him from the first moment in the
morning until the last moment at night. "From the
rising of the sun unto the *going down* of the same the
Lord's name is to be praised" (Psalm 113:3, *KJV*). We
should praise the Lord every day, all day long. "My
mouth shall be filled with Your praise and with Your
honor *all the day*" (Psalm 71:8, *AMP*).

No matter what is going wrong in our lives, we
have so much to praise the Lord for! We should praise
the Lord and thank Him continually because Jesus
came to earth and paid the tremendous price that will
enable all Christians who have been reborn spiritually to live eternally in the paradise of heaven. No
matter what we're going through now, our hearts
should *sing with* joy at this glorious prospect and this
abundance of joy in our hearts should come out of our
mouths in the form of continual praise to Almighty
God.

Some Christians seldom open their mouths to
praise the Lord. We are called to a life of praise and
we should continually offer up the sacrifice of praise.
This is *especially* true when the Lord allows us to go

100

through difficult times. If we praise the Lord during these times, He will preserve us and keep us from slipping. He will bring us through our problems to a place of abundance:

"Praise our God, O peoples, *let the sound of his praise be heard;* he has *preserved our lives* and *kept our feet from slipping.* For you, O God, *tested us;* you *refined us* like silver. You brought us *into prison* and laid *burdens* on our backs. You let men *ride over our heads;* we *went through fire and water,* but you *brought us to a place of abundance*" (Psalm 66:8-12, *NIV*).

Gold and silver are purified by the heat of fire. We are purified by praising the Lord in the midst of adversity. As we praise Him continually in the midst of our problems, the things that separate us from Him are burned away and our relationship with Him becomes much more pure and beautiful. "As the refining pot for silver and the furnace of gold [bring forth all the impurities of the metal], *so let a man be in his trial of praise* [ridding it of *all* that is base or insincere] — for a man is judged by what he praises..." (Proverbs 27:21, *AMP*).

Praise lightens the load. Continual praise in the face of pressure will *reduce* the effect of the pressure. Satan wants us to be sad and melancholy when we're going through hard times. He has evil spirits who try to put their dark clouds all around us when the going is tough. How do we get rid of this darkness and gloom?

We do this by praising the Lord continually. Our Father has given us praise to *cover us* from these attacks of the enemy. He wants us to *wrap this praise around us* like a garment — to cover ourselves with it at all times. When we do this, we will *rid ourselves* of Satan's dark clouds of despair. We will make a "trade" — "...*the garment* [expressive] of praise instead of a heavy, burdened and failing spirit..." (Isaiah 61:3, *AMP*).

If we are depressed and discouraged, we are *not* manifesting the victory that Jesus has given to us. We should *give* the discouragement, depression and despair *to Him*. We do this by *praising Him* continually. The worse our problems are, the *more* we need to praise Him.

If we praise the Lord and keep on praising Him, Satan's dark cloud of gloom will lift and go away. Continual praise brings us *out* of the problem *into* the solution and *into* the blessings of God. "Let the people praise thee, O God; let *all* the people praise thee. *Then shall the earth yield her increase; and God, even our own God, shall bless us*" (Psalm 67:5-6, *KJV*).

This analogy of the earth yielding an increase shows us that, when we praise the Lord, we are actually *sowing seeds*. Our Father's Word tells us that we will reap what we sow. If we sow little or no seeds of praise, we won't reap much of a harvest of blessing. However, if we praise the Lord continually, we will receive *great blessings*. "He which soweth *sparingly* shall reap also *sparingly*; and he which soweth *bountifully* shall reap also *bountifully*" (II Corinthians 9:6, *KJV*).

When we praise the Lord continually, this *releases* the faith that we already have and helps us to build *more* faith. *Continual praise changes fear into faith.* When the bottom seems to be falling out, *this* is the time to praise the Lord and to boldly speak the promises from His Word.

The more we do this, the more our faith grows because our ears continually hear *our mouths* boldly praising the Lord and boldly speaking His Word. "...faith cometh by *hearing*, and hearing by the Word of God" (Romans 10:17, *KJV*).

We *cannot* praise the Lord continually and remain discouraged. Praise *drives out* despair and brings us help from God. "*Why* are you in despair, O my soul? And *why* have you become disturbed within me? Hope in God, for I shall again *praise Him* for the help of His presence" (Psalm 42:5, NASV).

The more we praise the Lord, the stronger our faith becomes. If our hearts are fixed and solidly established, praise will pour out of our mouths. "My heart is *fixed*, O God, my heart is *fixed: I will sing and give praise*" (Psalm 57:7, KJV).

If we have filled our hearts with God's Word and trust completely in Him, praise will continually pour out of our mouths. "Because Your loving-kindness is better than life, my lips shall praise You" (Psalm 63:3, AMP). Continual praise transforms the adversity that we face into a blessing from the Lord and our weakness is transformed into God's strength. Continual praise in the face of adversity opens the door for miracles to happen.

When violent wind storms hit trees, they bend. If their roots are deep enough, they are able to ride out the storm and continue on stronger than ever. The same principle applies to us. If our hearts are filled with God's Word, our deep-rooted faith will manifest itself as we boldly praise the Lord and speak His promises when we are in the midst of life's storms. When we do this, we may bend, but we won't break. We'll ride out the storms and come through them stronger than ever.

It's easy to focus continually on the problem. It's easy to give in. It's not easy to keep our eyes off the problem and on the Lord. It's not easy to praise the Lord continually in the face of severe adversity. However, the easy way seldom is the right way.

When we praise the Lord continually when most

people couldn't see one solitary reason for praising Him, these words of faith and praise bring us into alignment with the Spirit of God living inside of us and open the door for His power to be released on our behalf. He will strengthen us and help us if we'll trust Him and lean confidently on Him. "The Lord is *my strength* and *my [impenetrable] shield;* my heart *trusts, relies on* and *confidently leans on Him,* and I am *helped*; therefore my heart greatly *rejoices,* and with my song will I *praise Him*" (Psalm 28:7, *AMP).*

When we continually praise the Lord in the face of adversity, this brings us into the presence of God. In the last chapter we saw that we entered into His gates with thanksgiving. Continual praise brings us *face to face* with Him. "Enter into his gates with thanksgiving, and *into his courts with praise...*" (Psalm 100:4, *KJV).*

A continual sacrifice of thanksgiving and praise opens spiritual doors that cannot be opened any other way. Continually speaking words of doubt and complaint open the door to Satan and bring us into his presence. Satan doesn't know what to do when he gives us his best shot and, instead of speaking words of fear and doubt, we boldly praise the Lord and claim His precious promises. The constant expression of praise is more than the satanic forces in the air around us can handle.

Our continuous praise shows Satan and his helpers that we haven't fallen for their bluffs. Jesus Christ is in complete control. His victory is our victory. He lives inside of us and is much, much more powerful than anything that Satan can use against us.

When we continually praise the Lord from deep down inside of our hearts, this brings us into His presence and our enemies — Satan and his evil spirits — *flee* because they *cannot stand* to be in the presence of Almighty God. "I *will praise thee*, O Lord, with my whole heart; I will show forth *all* thy marvelous works. I will be *glad* and *rejoice* in thee: I will *sing praise* to thy name, O thou most High. *When mine enemies are turned back, they shall fall and perish at thy presence*" (Psalm 9:1-3, *KJV*).

The closer we are to the Lord, the more we will praise Him. In fact, it is virtually impossible to be very close to the Lord and not praise Him continually. Genuine praise isn't something that we "manufacture." It is born out of a close walk with the Lord. The closer we are to Him, the more praise will flow out of our mouths because of our overwhelming faith in His magnificence.

It isn't easy for some people to praise the Lord. Satan tries to make us think that people who continually praise the Lord are fanatics. God's Word says that we are "peculiar" — a unique, different and special group of people — "...ye are a chosen generation, a royal priesthood, an holy nation, *a peculiar people*; that ye should *show forth the praises* of him who hath called you out of darkness into his marvellous light: which in time past were not a people, but are now the people of God: which had not obtained mercy, but now have obtained mercy" (I Peter 2:9-10, *KJV*).

If we comprehend the magnificent mercy that we have received and how God has taken us out of Satan's horrible darkness into His own wonderful light, praise *will* flow out of our mouths. We are now God's *special chosen people*. We are part of the *royal family* of Almighty God and *we will live eternally* with Him in heaven. Once we begin to understand these great truths, it is very difficult *not* to praise Him continually.

However, some Christians find that it is very

unnatural to praise the Lord. Because their lives have changed very little, if at all, they find it very difficult to praise the Lord continually or to understand those who do. Our carnal, prideful self has a natural tendency to want to do things *our* way. Continual praise of the Lord comes out of a transformed, humble nature.

We see a wonderful example of praise at the birth of Jesus. When He was born in Bethlehem, an angel appeared that night before shepherds in a field and told them about the birth of the Messiah. Suddenly this angel was surrounded by hundreds of other angels all praising God. "...suddenly there appeared with the angel an army of the troops of heaven — a heavenly knighthood — *praising God* and saying, Glory to God in the highest [heaven], and on earth peace among men with whom He is well-pleased — men of good will, of His favor" (Luke 2:13-14, *AMP*).

On that first Christmas, a vast multitude of angels praised God. Even though we can't see it with our human eyes or hear it with our human ears, the atmosphere around us is continually filled with angelic praise. As we, too, praise the Lord continually, *we loose the power of these angels* to minister to and on our behalf and we *bind Satan's fallen angels* from working against us.

We should get used to praising the Lord. When we get to heaven, we're going to be in the midst of a continual symphony of praise. When John received his revelation of heaven, he said, "...I heard the shouting of a vast crowd in heaven, *'Hallelujah! Praise the Lord!...'*" (Revelation 19:1, *TLB*).

In heaven, large crowds continually praise the Lord. This is beyond our limited human comprehension. John described praise in heaven when He said, "I heard again what sounded like the shouting of a huge crowd, or like the waves of a hundred oceans crashing on the shore, or like the mighty rolling of great thunder, '*Praise the Lord*. For the Lord our God, the Almighty, reigns...'" (Revelation 19:6, *TLB)*.

Angels all around us are praising the Lord. Everyone in heaven is praising the Lord. We should follow their example and praise the Lord continually here on earth.

Every day I try to praise the Lord continually and rejoice in Him, boldly saying such things as, "Thank you, Jesus. Praise you, Lord. Hallelujah. I glorify you, Wonderful Lord. You are everything. I am nothing. You are strong. I am weak. I can do all things in your strength. I worship you. I exalt you. I magnify you. I love you. Thank you for your grace, your love, your mercy, your kindness and your wisdom."

This praise and worship starts when I first get up in the morning and keeps coming out throughout the day. When things are going bad, I try to praise Him even more. I can recall many instances of praising the Lord where tears streamed down my face. I can remember praising the Lord continually when my body was racked with pain and on other occasions when my whole world seemed to be falling apart because of severe personal problems.

When we praise the Lord continually, we give Him the glory that He deserves, instead of withholding the glory that is due Him and keeping it for ourselves. "He who brings an *offering* of praise and thanksgiving *honors and glorifies Me...*" (Psalm 50:23, *AMP)*.

We aren't doing God any "favor" by praising Him. He is completely worthy of our praises and, as we give Him the praise that He deserves, He uses this praise to save us from our enemies. "I call upon the Lord, who is *worthy* to be praised, and *I am saved from my enemies*" (Psalm 18:3, *NASV)*.

God's ways are much different from the world's ways. When we are faced with adversity, it is very important for us to praise the Lord continually. When we do this, we open the door for the Lord to minister to us during our trials and then to bring us safely through these trials.

Chapter 14
The Power Of Prayer

One of the very best things that we can do when we're faced with severe adversity is to spend a great deal of time in prayer. Our Father is delighted when His children come to Him in prayer. "...the prayer of the upright is His *delight!*" (Proverbs 15:8, *AMP*). When the going is tough, *instead* of getting discouraged and giving up, we should pray *continually.* "...they ought *always to pray* and *not* to turn coward — faint, lose heart and give up" (Luke 18:1, *AMP*).

Again and again, God's Word tells us to pray continually. *"Be unceasing in prayer — praying perseveringly..."* (I Thessalonians 5:17, *AMP*). When we're faced with adversity, we need to pray patiently and continually. "...Be patient in trouble, and prayerful *always"* (Romans 12:12, *TLB*).

When we are so weak that we can't get the job done, we should continually turn to the presence of the One who can do all things. "Seek the Lord and His strength, yearn for and seek His face and to be in His presence *continually!"* (I Chronicles 16:11, *AMP*).

He wants us to turn to Him throughout the day and night. "...I will call upon God; and the Lord shall save me. *Evening*, and *morning*, and *at noon*, will I pray, and cry aloud: and he *shall* hear my voice. *He hath delivered my soul in peace from the battle that was against me..."* (Psalm 55:16-18, *KJV*).

When we are reborn spiritually, this brings us into right standing with God and makes us righteous in His sight. When God's righteous children pray earnestly and continually, our prayers *release* the power of Almighty God. "...*The earnest (heartfelt, continued) prayer of a righteous man makes tremendous power available — dynamic in its working*" (James 5:16, *AMP*).

Our Father is never too busy to hear our prayer. When we need help from a doctor or dentist, sometimes we have to wait several days in order to get an appointment. Even though millions of prayers may be going up to Him at the same time that we pray, we *won't* get any "busy signals." "Call to Me, *and I will answer you...*" (Jeremiah 33:3, *NASV*). He hears the prayers of His children who approach Him reverently and do His will. "...if any one is God-fearing and a worshipper of Him and does His will, *He listens to him*" (John 9:31, *AMP*). *If we know that God hears our prayers, doesn't it make a lot of sense to pray continually to Him????*

The *key* to receiving an answer to our prayers is to pray according to God's will. If our prayer is in line with His will, we *know* that He hears us and we *know* that He will answer. "This is the confidence we have in approaching God: that if we ask *anything according to his will*, he hears us. And if we *know* that he hears us — *whatever* we ask — we *know* that we *have* what we asked of him" (I John 5:14, *NIV*).

Sometimes God's will is not the same as ours. When we pray, many of us pray according to *our* wants and desires *instead of* continually seeking *God's will*. We *shouldn't* pray to get *our* will done in heaven. Our prayers should be in order to get *our Father's* will done here on earth.

Our lives should be devoted to finding His will and doing what *He* wants us to do, *not* what *we* want to do. If we really do this, our prayers *will* be answered. "...we receive from Him *whatever we ask for, because*

110

we (watchfully) *obey* His orders — *observe* His suggestions and injunctions, *follow* His plan for us — and (habitually) *practice* what is *pleasing* to Him" (I John 3:22, *AMP*).

It is very important to pray to our Father based upon His Word. God's Word and His will are one and the same. Our prayer requests should be based upon a promise from His Word. "...I will pray unto the Lord your God *according to your words*; and it *shall* come to pass..." (Jeremiah 42:4, *KJV*).

Our Father wants us to pray the answer, not the problem. We can identify the problem when we pray, but the majority of our prayer time should be based upon the answer from His Word, claiming this promise in answer to our prayer and thanking Him for answering based upon the promise that He has given us. Our Father will *always* do His part. *Will we* do *our* part?

His part is to give us whatever we ask for according to His will. *Our part* is to continually seek His will for our lives and to do what He wants us to do. *If* our lives are completely surrendered to God's will and *if* we trust completely in Him, *every one* of our prayers will be answered. "...*whatever* you ask for in prayer, having *faith* and [*really*] *believing*, you *will* receive" (Matthew 21:22, *AMP*).

Satan is terrified when He hears us continually approaching our Father with a prayer of faith that is in His will. If we pray continually according to the will of God and if our faith persists and absolutely refuses to waver between the time we pray and the time the answer is manifested, Satan knows that God will answer every time.

There is no prayer that our Father cannot and will not answer as long as our faith is strong and enduring and the prayer is in His will. This is very discouraging to Satan because he knows that he can't have any lasting effect on us if we know how to pray properly. So, he does everything that he can to stop us from learning to do this. Jesus taught us to always pray directly to our Father and to always pray in the name of Jesus. "...you won't need to ask me for anything, for you can go *directly* to the Father and ask him, and he *will* give you what you ask for *because you use my name*" (John 16:23, *TLB).*

The name of Jesus Christ has immense spiritual power. His name was not picked out by Mary and Joseph. God sent an angel to Joseph to tell him the name that He had chosen. "...an angel of the Lord appeared to him in a dream, saying, Joseph, descendant of David, do not be afraid to take Mary [as] your wife, for that which is conceived in her is of (from, out of) the Holy Spirit. She will bear a Son, *and you shall call His name Jesus* [in Hebrew means Savior]..." (Matthew 1:20-21, *AMP).*

God gave Him that name, and the power of that name is *so great* in the spiritual realm that *everyone everywhere must* kneel before it. "...God has highly exalted Him and has freely bestowed on Him the name that is *above every name,* that in (at) the name of Jesus *every knee should (must) bow,* in heaven and on earth and under the earth, and *every* tongue [frankly and openly] *confess* and *acknowledge* that Jesus Christ is Lord..." (Philippians 2:9-11, *AMP).*

In the spiritual realm, Jesus and His name are one and the same. The name of Jesus gives us power in three separate realms—above the earth, on the earth and under the earth. We should have strong, dominating, unwavering faith in the name of Jesus. We should speak it boldly and often every day of our lives and we should use it continually as we pray.

His name keeps us safe. "The name of the Lord is a

strong tower: the righteous runneth into it, and is *safe*"
(Proverbs 18:10, *KJV*). Our Father *blesses* us when we
come to Him in the name of Jesus. "*Blessed* is he that
cometh in the name of the`Lord" (Luke 13:35, *KJV*).

If someone goes to the bank with a signed check
drawn upon our account, the bank will cash this
check if there is enough money in the account. The
signature on the check releases the money that is on
deposit. The name of Jesus is the "*signature*" that
releases answers to God. When we go to our Father in
prayer in the name of Jesus and pray according to
His will with strong, persistent, unwavering faith, we
will release the answer in the spiritual realm and
bring it into manifestation in the natural realm.

We can't approach our Father in our *own* righteousness, but we *can* approach Him through *Jesus*.
Because of the price that Jesus paid at Calvary, we
can approach our Father any time in the name of
Jesus and, in the spiritual realm, He treats this the
same as if Jesus Himself approached Him.

When we pray to the Father in Jesus' name, Jesus
is the intermediary between God and ourselves. He is
our mediator. "...there is one God, and *one mediator*
between God and men, the man Christ Jesus..." (I
Timothy 2:5, *KJV*). Jesus represents us to the Father
when we pray. Just as a lawyer represents his clients,
Jesus intercedes on our behalf. "...we have an Advocate (One Who *will intercede* for us) with the Father;
[it is] Jesus Christ [the all] righteous — upright, just,
Who *conforms* to the Father's will in *every* purpose,
thought and action" (I John 2:1, *AMP*).

Isn't it comforting when we pray to our Father in
Jesus' name to know that Jesus Christ, the righteous
One who always conforms to our Father's will, is
interceding on our behalf? When we pray to God,
Jesus represents us to our Father. He pleads on our

behalf. He is always available to intercede for us. "...He is *always* living to *make petition* to God and *intercede* with Him and *intervene* for them" (Hebrews 7:25, *AMP*). When we pray the prayer of faith according to God's will and we pray in the name of Jesus, we *know* that Jesus is representing us to God.

If our lives truly are *centered* around the Lord and if our hearts are *full of* God's Word, our prayers will be answered. *"If you live in Me — abide vitally united to Me — and My words remain in you and continue to live in your hearts, ask whatever you will and it shall be done for you"* (John 15:7, *AMP*).

This is how God teaches us to pray. We should pray continually and fervently based upon His will and the promises in His Word. We should pray in the name of Jesus Christ who intercedes for us. We should come boldly to our Father. This brings us to the final step of all prayer: bringing the answer from the spiritual realm into manifestation in the natural realm.

There is *no such thing* as a prayer in the will of God and backed by deep, unwavering, persistent faith that goes unanswered. These prayers are answered *immediately* in the spiritual realm. However, there is often a *delay* between the time we receive the answer in the spiritual realm and the time this answer is manifested in the natural realm.

As always, God *will* do *His* part. *Will* we do our part?? During this period of time between our prayer and the manifestation of its answer, our part is to maintain a steady, unwavering persevering faith. Our words and actions should be exactly the same as they would be if the answer had already been received.

We must not let doubting words come out of our mouths. We need to hold fast our confession of faith in the Lord. "...let us *hold fast* our confession [of faith in Him]..." (Hebrews 4:14, *AMP*). If our faith, words and

114

actions are strong and persistent, in God's timing this faith will reach into the spiritual realm like a huge magnet and draw the manifestation into the natural realm.

Satan's evil spirits do everything that they possibly can to get in the way and delay the manifestation of these answers. They hope that, by delaying the answers, we will get *discouraged* and *open our mouths to voice our discouragement,* thus *blocking or delaying* the manifestation of God's answer by verbally acknowledging our lack of faith.

When we pray, believing according to God's will, our prayers activate angels. Our words during the period while we are waiting for the manifestation give power to these angels in the air around us. It is very important to continually speak God's Word with faith in order to keep His angels working for us. "...you His angels, you mighty ones who do His commandments, *hearkening to the voice of His word*" (Psalm 103:20, *AMP*).

Let's close this chapter on prayer by discussing the subject of intercessory prayer. Intercessory prayer is especially important to us when we are going through adversity. "...keep alert and watch with strong purpose and perseverance, *interceding in behalf of all the saints* (God's consecrated people)" (Ephesians 6:18, *AMP*).

When I have a problem, I often ask one or two people to pray for me — people with strong faith who are especially close to me. If I have a very big problem, I ask *many* people to pray for me. Nothing gives me more comfort when I am going through a very difficult time than to know that several other people are interceding for me on a continuing basis.

In our church, we have a prayer chain. If anyone needs intercessory prayer, they call in their need and immediately this is telephoned to key people on the prayer chain who, in turn, immediately call other members of the prayer chain. Within a few minutes, dozens of people will be interceding in prayer. This is very effective and we have heard many excellent testimonies of favorable results.

Intercessory prayer has tremendous power. We see an excellent example of this in the twelfth chapter of Acts which tells how King Herod had the apostle Peter arrested during the Passover celebration. He placed Peter under the guard of sixteen soldiers to hold him until the Passover celebration was completed. Peter then was to be executed.

The other Christians knew that they couldn't get past the sixteen soldiers. So, they prayed fervently and continually for Peter. "...*earnest prayer was going up* to God from the Church for his safety *all the time* he was in prison" (Acts 12:5, *TLB*).

Verses 6 through 17 tell us that the night before Peter was supposed to be executed he was sound asleep. While he slept he was double-chained between two soldiers with other soldiers standing guard. Suddenly an angel appeared and woke Peter up. The chains fell off Peter's wrists. The angel then led Peter out of the cell block and took him to the main gate of the prison which opened up and out they walked! Then the angel left.

Peter then went to a home where a prayer meeting was being held. All of the Christians there were astounded to see that their prayers were answered. We shouldn't ever underestimate the power of earnest, continued intercessory prayer. *It works!!*

In our early months as Christians, we pray a lot for ourselves and our families. However, as we grow and mature in the Lord, we'll realize how important it is to pray continually for other people. Even when I am in the midst of severe adversity, I spend almost all of my prayer time interceding for others. I seldom pray for my needs until after I have finished interceding for others. God not only blesses those whom we pray for, but He also blesses Christians who pray continually for others. We see a good example of this in the life of Job.

He suffered tremendously. The turning point that ended Job's season of suffering was His prayer for others. Even though He was going through a terrible ordeal, Job still prayed for others. "...the Lord turned the captivity of Job and restored his fortunes, *when he prayed for his friends...*" (Job 42:10, *AMP*).

All Christians should spend a considerable amount of time in intercessory prayer. Jesus intercedes for us before the Father. He wants us to do the same, interceding continually for others. We should pray for everyone who we know is going through problems. We should intercede continually for our church, for the pastor, the staff, the leaders of the church and all members of the church. We should pray continually for all people holding political office — including those government officials whose political beliefs are different from our own.

We should pray for the unsaved people in the world, for Christians in countries where religious freedom is restricted and for all Christian missionaries, evangelists and clergymen. We should pray each day for suffering people who we read about in our newspapers or see on television newscasts.

Great results come from continually interceding for others. They receive blessings as a result of our fervent intercessory prayer. God won't forget to bless us either.

Chapter 15
Giving Our Problems To The Lord

Our heavenly Father wants us to use the abilities that He has given us to do the very best that we can. "Whatever your hand finds to do, *do it with all your might...*" (Ecclesiastes 9:10, NIV). Whatever we are called to do should be done with every bit of ability that we possess as if we were working for the Lord Himself. "Whatever you do, work at it *with all your heart, as working for the Lord...*" (Colossians 3:23, NIV).

However, too many of us try to take responsibilities upon ourselves that belong to God. He doesn't want us trusting in our human abilities. Once we have done our very best, He wants us to stop struggling and straining. He is Almighty God. He wants us to trust in Him. *"Cease striving and know that I am God..."* (Psalm 46:10, NASV).

Don't we know who He is? He is our Creator. He created each of us and everything else in the entire universe. If He was able to create us and everything around us, doesn't it make sense to believe that He can easily solve any problem that confronts us???

Of course He can — *if we'll let him* — if we'll *stop* struggling and straining and *let go* of the problem, *trusting completely* in Him to solve it. Once we have done everything we can, we need to let go and stand firmly on our faith in Him. "...and having *done all* [the crisis demands], to *stand* [*firmly* in your place]" (Ephesians 6:13, AMP).

When we don't know what to do, God always knows what to do. When we can't see any way out of our problem, He can see *many* ways out. He knows His way through every twist and turn in the road of life. Once we have done our best, why should any of us ever worry if we *know* that He is there waiting — ready, willing and able to solve our problems *if* we'll just let go and trust Him?

In the natural realm, if our automobile is in bad shape and we don't know how to fix it, we take it to a mechanic. We need to do the same thing in the spiritual realm. When we're faced with a problem that we can't handle, we need to take the problem to the One who can handle it.

We need to let go of the trouble and trust the Expert One to take care of it for us. If we do this, He will show us exactly how He wants us to think and exactly what He wants us to do in order to succeed. "Roll your works upon the Lord — commit and trust them *wholly* to Him; [*He will cause your thoughts to become agreeable to His will*, and] so shall your plans be *established* and *succeed*" (Proverbs 16:3, *AMP*).

No matter what happens to us, the Lord *can* and *will* take care of it for us if we, (a) *commit* the problem totally to Him and, (b) *trust* completely in Him. "*Commit* your way to the Lord — roll and repose [each care of] your load on Him; *trust* (lean on, rely on and be confident) also in Him, *and He will bring it to pass*" (Psalm 37:5, *AMP*).

When we send a package to someone, we give it to the post office or the parcel service and forget about it. We don't worry whether or not it will be delivered. We need to do the same thing with the problems that we give to the Lord. *We need to let go and trust Him to deliver just as His Word says He will.*

If we do our part, He will always do His part. Our part is to *commit* the problem totally to Him, *trusting* completely in Him. His part is to *solve* the problem.

He can and will take care of everything if we'll just let Him.

Committing something to the Lord is a continuous process — not a one-day occurrence. We need to give Him the problem and *leave* it with Him. If we don't get an answer right away, *will we take it back* and try to handle everything ourselves? Or, *will we leave it with Him*, trusting quietly and confidently in Him even though we don't see any immediate solution?

We are very wrong if we try to do our Father's work for Him! Just think how ridiculous it is for one little human being vainly trying to do the work of God, the Creator of the entire universe. *"...trust yourself* to the God who made you, *for he will never fail you"* (1 Peter 4:19, *TLB*).

Of course we can trust completely in our Father! His Word says, "If anyone does not provide for his relatives, and especially for his immediate family, he has denied the faith and is worse than an unbeliever" (I Timothy 5:8, *NIV*). We are members of God's family. If He doesn't provide for us, then He is denying His own Word. If He sets this kind of standard for *earthly families*, then doesn't it make sense that we can trust Him to provide completely for *His family?*

We can trust completely in Him. He will always come through. He will always do exactly what His Word says He will do *unless* we deny Him through lack of faith. We need to release the weight. We need to stop trying to carry the load. The Lord will hold us up if we'll let go and not take it back because we trust Him. He won't ever let us go under. "Cast your burden on the Lord [*releasing* the weight of it] and He *will* sustain you; He will *never* allow the [consistently] righteous to be moved — made to slip, fall or fail" (Psalm 55:22, *AMP*).

Note the words "consistently righteous." We need to do *more* than just come into right standing with God. We need to *stay there*, always putting Him first in our lives. Only when we do this will we be able to trust Him enough to give Him our loads and not take them back if He doesn't answer right away.

He wants *all* of our worries, fears and concerns. He wants us to give *all* of them to Him, trusting completely in Him. *He cares very much* about what happens to us and He will never let us down if we'll just let go and trust completely in Him. "Casting the *whole* of your care — *all* your anxieties, *all* your worries, *all* your concerns, *once and for all*—on Him; for *He cares for you affectionately, and cares about you watchfully*" (I Peter 5:7, *AMP*).

We shouldn't have any worries, anxieties or cares of any kind. If we do what God's Word tells us to do, we will cast *all* of our cares on Him. Then we'll be carefree — completely free of all worries, anxieties and cares because we have given all of them to the Lord.

He knows the way out. He wants us to let go and place our weight completely on Him. If we do, He will guide us. "...on You do I *lean* and in You do I *trust*. Cause me to know the way wherein I should walk, for I lift up my inner self to You" (Psalm 143:8, *AMP*).

We *don't* need to carry many of the loads that we are trying to carry. Jesus has *already* carried our grief and sorrow for us. "*Surely he hath borne our griefs, and carried our sorrows...*" (Isaiah 53:4, *KJV*). If Jesus has already carried them, we *don't* have to carry them again.

To illustrate this point, imagine going to a store, placing an order and paying the purchase price when we placed the order. What would we do if we went to pick up the order and the clerk told us that we owed them money? We'd deny this and show our receipt, wouldn't we?

This is *exactly* what we should do when we're going through difficult times. We *don't* have to pay the price of carrying grief and sorrow. *This price has already been paid. Isaiah 53:4 is our receipt.* If we are carrying a load of grief and sorrow, we are carrying a load that our Lord *doesn't* want us to carry. He wants us to give our grief and sorrow to Him and walk away, leaving them with Him.

No matter what we go through, Jesus has been there first. He blazed the trail for us. He knows exactly what we're going through. We all know that Jesus carried our sins to the cross, but *we also need to know that He carried our sorrows to the cross.* He carried our heavy loads and said that He will give us rest. "Come to Me, all you who *labor* and are *heavy-laden* and *over burdened,* and I *will* cause you to rest— I *will* ease and relieve and refresh your souls" (Matthew 11:28, *AMP).*

First of all, He said "Come to Me." He *will* give us rest from our burdens, but we have to *willingly* give them to Him and leave them with Him. He is waiting. *He wants* to carry the load for us, but *He won't force us* to give it to Him. He *won't* interfere with our freedom of choice.

If we think that we have to take care of everything, He will let us. Many times the *only* way that He can get us to come to Him is to allow us to be knocked *so low* as a result of our pride and self-sufficiency that we are *more than willing* to give our problems to Him.

How do we give our loads to Jesus? The next two verses of Scripture give us the answer. "Take My yoke upon you, and learn of Me; for I am gentle (meek) and humble (lowly) in heart, and you will find rest — relief, ease and refreshment and recreation and blessed quiet — for your souls. For My yoke is wholesome (useful, good) — not harsh, hard, sharp or pressing, but comfortable, gracious and pleasant; and My burden is light and easy to be borne" (Matthew 11:29-30, *AMP*).

The key to understanding these two verses of Scripture is the word "yoke." Visualize a pair of oxen who are joined together by a wooden yoke — a frame that fits around their necks. This yoke binds them together and prohibits individual freedom of movement. They are under the complete control of the person who controls the yoke. *This* is what Jesus wants us to do. He wants us to *get into His yoke, to give up our freedom* to do things *our* way and, instead, to *willingly* give control of our lives to *Him.*

When we get into His yoke, *then* we will be able to rest because we have *stopped* struggling and straining, trying to solve our problems. We *let go* of them and give them to Him when we get into His yoke, trusting completely in Him to carry the load for us.

Jesus tells us *how* to get into this yoke. *We do this by being meek and humble, just as He is* — by realizing that we *can't* solve many of the problems that we are confronted with and *humbly acknowledging* that, if He doesn't solve them for us, they *aren't* going to get solved.

Faith starts with humility. *Humility says,* "I know that I can't solve this. I don't know how to solve this. I'm totally helpless." *Faith says,* "I can't solve it, but I know that the Lord can and I know that He will. I give this problem to Him. I trust completely in Him."

This is how we enter into the yoke of Jesus Christ. *This* is how we find an answer to the problems that are so heavy that we can't carry them. Jesus never gets tired. He never gets discouraged. He never gives up. He *already has* the victory. No matter how heavy our burdens might be to us, they are light to Him. He is fully able to carry all of the problems we have ever had, all of the problems we have now and all of the problems we ever will have.

The burdens that are so heavy for us are as light as a feather to Him. We are *so foolish* if we try to carry these burdens ourselves! God didn't mean for us to carry the burdens that many of us are trying to carry. Often, we are trying to solve problems that only the Lord can solve.

We need to relax and let Him take care of it for us. "The Lord *will fight for you*, and you shall *hold your peace* and *remain at rest*" (Exodus 14:14, *AMP*). We must not try to fight the battles that are the Lord's battles, not ours. "...*the battle is not yours but God's*" (II Chronicles 20:15, *AMP*).

He doesn't need us to fight His battles for Him!!! He wants us to do the best we can and then He wants us to *let go*! It's *not* our fight, it is *His* fight. *Our fight is to "fight the good fight of faith..."* (I Timothy 6:12, *KJV*).

It is a *good* fight because we *know* that we will win *if* we'll let go and trust completely in the Lord. God knows how to fight and win battles that we can't possibly win. The only thing that can stop Him is if we refuse to give Him the problem and leave it with Him, trusting in Him.

Jesus has already fought every battle for us. We will come out winners if we believe completely in the total victory that He gave us and endure with total faith in Him until the manifestation of His victory is brought from the spiritual realm into the natural realm.

Chapter 16
God's Strength — Not Ours

One of the reasons why our Father allows us to go through seasons of adversity is to cause us to increase our spiritual strength. Most of us have seen people who were able to reach down inside of themselves to obtain extra strength while they were going through a crisis. This should be especially true of Christians. The Lord has made a great deal of extra strength available to us.

Unfortunately, the world that we live in places most of its emphasis on *human* strength and little or no emphasis on *spiritual* strength. All of us have heard worldly sayings such as, "When the going gets tough, the tough get going." In the world there are many training courses, books and recordings on subjects such as *self*-confidence, *self*-reliance, *self*-awareness and *self*-image.

All of these things sound good, but they are *not* scriptural. The Word of God teaches *Christ*-confidence, *Christ*-reliance, and *Christ*-awareness. It teaches that the way to improve our self-image is to focus on Jesus Christ living inside of us.

As we read the following words that come out of the mouth of the greatest person who ever lived, we'll see how *different* God's ways are from the self-centered, self-confident ways that the world teaches. Jesus Christ said these words:

"...The Son can do nothing of himself..." (John 5:19, *KJV*).

"I can of mine own self do *nothing*..." (John 5:30, *KJV*).

"...I seek *not* mine *own* will, but the will of the Father which hath sent me" (John 5:30, *KJV*).

"Do you not believe that I am in the Father and that the Father is in Me? What I am telling you *I do not say on My own authority and of My own* accord, but *the Father Who lives continually in Me does the works — His* miracles, His own deeds of power" (John 14:10, *AMP*).

We can clearly see that Jesus Christ, the perfect Man who lived the perfect life, did *not* trust in His own ability. His life, which is the model for us, depended *not* on His human strength and ability, but on the strength and ability of God living inside of Him.

It is very important for us to apply this principle in our lives. Our Father gave us human abilities to handle the normal, everyday decisions of life. However, He *never* intended for us to use these limited human abilities to solve extremely serious problems that can only be solved in the spiritual realm.

For example, no thinking person would ever try to outrace a speeding automobile or try to fly by his own power. In the same manner, we should realize what we can do with our limited human abilities and when we can't go further on our own strength.

Some people are able to accomplish a great deal with their human ability. In truth, this great human ability is usually a *liability*, not an asset. This tends to give these people *too much* confidence in their own strength and ability. No matter how strong our human strength and ability might be, it lasts only for a season. Sooner or later, all of us will get to the point where we can't solve our problems with our own abilities. "...*let him that thinketh he standeth take heed lest he fall*" (I Corinthians 10:12, *KJV*).

Satan loves to see us trusting in our own strength. He knows that God's Word says, "...by strength shall *no* man prevail" (I Samuel 2:9, *KJV*). No matter how strong we are, sooner or later we'll come up against more than we can handle. "...a mighty man is *not* delivered by much strength" (Psalm 33:16, *KJV*).

Why should Christians depend on human strength when supernatural strength is available to us? If we depend only on ourselves and other human beings, we are headed for big problems sooner or later. If we place our trust in the Lord, we'll receive great blessings:

"Thus says the Lord: *Cursed* [with great evil] is the strong man who trusts and relies on frail man, making weak [human] *flesh* his arm, and whose mind and heart turn aside from the Lord. For he shall be like a shrub or a person naked and destitute in the desert, and shall not see any good come; but shall dwell in the parched places in the wilderness, in uninhabited salt land. [*Most*] *blessed* is the man who believes in, trusts in and relies on the Lord, and whose hope and confidence *the Lord is*. For he shall be like a tree planted by the waters, that spreads out its roots by the river, and shall not see and fear when heat comes, but his leaf shall be green; he shall not be anxious and careful in the year of drought, nor shall he cease from yielding fruit" (Jeremiah 17:5-8, *AMP*).

God's weakness is stronger than the strength of any human being. "...the *foolishness* of God is *wiser* than man's wisdom, and the *weakness* of God is *stronger* than man's strength" (I Corinthians 1:25, *NIV*). We can't accomplish anything in the spiritual realm without Jesus Christ. "...apart from Me — cut off from vital union with Me — you can do *nothing*"

127

(John 15:5, *AMP*). We can't do anything in the spiritual realm without Jesus, but we can do all things through Him. "...I have strength for *all* things in Christ Who empowers me — I am ready for anything and equal to *anything* through Him Who infuses inner strength into me, [that is, I am self-sufficient in Christ's sufficiency]" (Philippians 4:13, *AMP*).

We should draw our strength from the unlimited strength that the Lord has made available to us. "...be strong *in the Lord* — be empowered through your union with Him; draw your strength *from Him* — that strength which His [boundless] might provides" (Ephesians 6:10, *AMP*).

Many of us get into trouble because we try to resist Satan with our human strength. Satan isn't worried in the least about our human abilities. He is always worried when we learn how to come at Him with the spiritual weapons the Lord has given us. "...the Lord *is* faithful and He *will* strengthen [you] and set you on a *firm foundation* and *guard you from the evil* [one]" (II Thessalonians 3:3, *AMP*). When we trust in His strength, there is *nothing* to fear. "...the Lord is the strength of my life; *of whom shall I be afraid?*" (Psalm 27:1, *KJV*).

We shouldn't ever say that we "can't" overcome a problem. This denies the Word of God which tells us that we can do all things through Jesus Christ. Through His strength we can go *through* any problem and we can climb *over* any problem. "...by thee I have run *through* a troop: by my God have I leaped *over* a wall" (II Samuel 22:30, *KJV*).

The strength of the Lord is available to us to the exact degree that we believe it is! His strength is not "automatic."As always is the case, God has done His part. He has provided us with the strength that we need. We need to do our part. Our part is to know what His Word says about the strength that is available to us and *then to step forth in faith based upon this.* "The Lord *is good,* a *strong hold* in the day of trouble; *and he knòweth them that trust in him*" (Nahum 1:7, *KJV*).

Our Father will help His children and give us strength *if* we trust Him. "...the salvation of the righteous is of the Lord: *he is their strength* in the time of trouble. And the Lord *shall help them, and deliver them:* he shall deliver them from the wicked, and *save them, because they trust in him*" (Psalm 37:39-40, *KJV*).

We build this trust by studying and meditating continually in God's Word. "*Seek* the Lord and His strength, yearn for and *seek* His face and to *be in His presence continually*!" (I Chronicles 16:11, *AMP*). When the going is tough, the strength that we need *is* available to us. It is in the Word of God. "My soul is weary with sorrow; *strengthen me according to your word*" (Psalm 119:28, *NIV*).

When the storms of life are beating on us, this is when it is very important to be alone with the Lord on a regular, continuing basis. Spiritual strength comes from solitude. It comes from many, many precious hours spent alone with the Lord, studying and meditating in His Word, praying, worshipping and fellowshipping with Him.

The more quiet time we spend alone with the Lord, the more His love, faith, peace, wisdom and strength will flow into us. As we do this continually, we will *more than replenish* the love, faith, peace, wisdom and strength that we spend dealing with the problems that we face.

Spiritual strength comes from knowing the Lord, from having *such* a close personal relationship with Him that we *know* He will strengthen us and guide us. "...the people who *know their* God shall prove themselves *strong* and shall stand *firm*..." (Daniel 11:32, *AMP*). The more we renew our minds in God's Word, the closer we will draw to Him and the more we will become like Him. "...put on the *new self*, which is being *renewed* in knowledge in the image of its Creator" (Colossians 3:10, *NIV*).

I ask each person reading this book — *do you* know *exactly* what you need to do for God's strength to be made absolutely perfect in your life? The answer is to stop trying to do everything with your own ability. God's strength is made perfect in the *last place* that the world ever would think of finding the greatest strength that there is. It is made perfect in *our weakness*. "...he said unto me, My grace is sufficient for thee: *for my strength is made perfect in weakness. Most gladly* therefore will I rather *glory in my* infirmities, that the power of Christ may rest upon me. *Therefore I take pleasure* in infirmities, in reproaches, in necessities, in persecutions, in distresses for Christ's sake: *for when I am weak, then am I strong*" (II Corinthians 12:9-10, *KJV*).

If we ever want to see a perfect example of how different God's ways are from man's ways, II Corinthians 12:9-10 is it. Worldly people would never look for strength in weakness. The carnal mind thinks it is absolutely stupid to take pleasure in our problems. Yet, God's Word tells us to do these two things.

Why should we "take pleasure" when we are faced with a problem that is much more than we can handle? The answer is that this is exactly when His perfect strength is released on our behalf! The truth is that we are strong when we trust the Lord and we are weak when we trust ourselves.

Human strength and ability actually are a *liability* because they tempt us to trust in ourselves. Human weakness is an *asset* if recognition of this weakness causes us to trust the Lord. *God's strength can only be released and made perfect when we trust Him in the midst of our weakness!*

Our heavenly Father isn't concerned with our shortcomings. He can more than compensate for any abilities that we might lack. He isn't looking for human abilities, strength and self-confidence. *He is looking for human weakness that dares to trust in Him and keep on trusting in Him no matter how bad our problems might seem to be.* This is incomprehensible to our limited human understanding, but this is a definite spiritual truth.

When we come to Him in our weakness and we can't go any further, our *faith* in Him will *trade* our weakness for His strength. "He gives *power* to the *faint* and *weary*, and to him who has *no might* He *increases strength* — causing it to *multiply* and making it *abound*" (Isaiah 40:29, *AMP*). We *release* the power of God's strength by admitting our weakness and trusting in God's strength. "...let the weak say, I am strong" (Joel 3:10, *KJV*).

Spiritual power is released by words. When we speak something, we give it power in the spiritual realm. When our backs are up against the wall and we can't go one step further, we should open our mouths and say, "Jesus, I'm weak. I can't handle this problem with my human strength and ability. I know this and I freely admit it. However, your Word says that I can do all things through your strength and that your strength is made perfect in my weakness. Therefore, I'm going to keep on going trusting completely in your strength."

When we believe this in our hearts, say this with deep conviction coming out of a believing heart and act accordingly, then the strength of the Lord is available to us. When we are weak, we should praise the Lord continually and thank Him for His wondrous strength that is available to us. Our Father searches for His children who believe this deep down in their hearts. "...the eyes of the Lord move to and fro throughout the earth that He may *strongly support* those whose heart is *completely His*..." (II Chronicles 16:9, *NASV*).

God is looking for something that is very rare — a human being who is admittedly weak and, in the midst of this weakness, will confess faith in God and actually step out in faith, knowing that His strength is made perfect in our weakness. Our Father wants *so much* to manifest His strength on our behalf, and He looks *continually* for His children who will trust *completely* in Him in the midst of our *admitted weakness*.

Our helplessness opens the door to God's help. The more we realize how helpless we really are, the more we open the channels for our Father to help us. In the world, people try to hide weakness and appear strong to win the admiration of other people. *Our Father wants us to do just the opposite.*

Again and again we should open our mouths and *admit* our weakness and speak His Word, boldly claiming the strength that He has made available to us. This repeated, enduring, unwavering confession of faith will release His strength on our behalf. We must not give up. When the going is tough, we need to open our mouths day after day to acknowledge our belief that His strength is released in our weakness.

He will give us the strength that we need one day at a time. "...*as thy days, so shall thy strength be*" (Deuteronomy 33:25, *KJV*). Our heavenly Father knows exactly how much strength we need and precisely when we need it. He will release this strength in direct proportion to our faith.

If we pray asking Him to remove a problem, He may do this or, in His wisdom, He may instead choose to give us the strength to bear up under the problem. We should trust completely in Him. We should rejoice in the tremendous victory of Jesus Christ, knowing that we have won over whatever comes against us.

Jesus *knows* that He has the victory. He *never* loses His joy. When we share this attitude and rejoice in the midst of adversity and joyously admit our weakness in the midst of adversity, this releases His joy and this gives us strength. *"...be not grieved and depressed, for the joy of the Lord is your strength and stronghold"* (Nehemiah 8:10, *AMP*).

The Lord's joy is our strength. This joy should flow through us every day of our lives *no matter* what problems we might be faced with. His joy will lift us above these problems and give us the strength to *overcome* them. *"...keep going no matter what happens— always full of the joy of the Lord..."* (Colossians 1:11, *TLB*).

Chapter 17
Almighty God Lives In Our Hearts

No study of God's Word on the subject of dealing with adversity would be complete without taking a careful look at our greatest asset: God Himself living inside of us. Most Christians have been taught that God is seated on His throne in heaven and that Jesus Christ sits at His right hand. This is true, but, by faith, God and Jesus *also* are available here on earth to live inside of us.

Almighty God Himself does live in our hearts. "One God and Father of all, who is above all, and through all, *and in you all*" (Ephesians 4:6, *KJV*). Jesus Christ does live in our hearts. "...Do you not yourselves realize and know (thoroughly by an ever-increasing experience) that *Jesus Christ is in you?...*" (II Corinthians 13:5, *AMP*). The Holy Spirit also lives in our hearts. "Do you not know that your body is the temple — the very sanctuary — of *the Holy Spirit Who lives within you...?*" (I Corinthians 6:19, *AMP*).

It's hard for our limited human understanding to understand that God and Jesus can sit side by side in heaven and, at the same time, live in the hearts of all Christian believers. God and Jesus are omnipresent. They can be in many different places at the same time.

There is no doubt that the *entire Trinity*, Father, Son and Holy Spirit, lives together in our hearts. "...in Christ you too are *filled with the Godhead: Father, Son* and *Holy Spirit*, and reach full spiritual stature..." (Colossians 2:10, *AMP*). *Isn't it wonderful to realize that God the Father, God the Son and God the*

Holy Spirit all live inside of us and go with us all day long, every place we go, every day of our lives?

We don't have a distant God who is far away from our trials and tribulations. Our God couldn't be closer. He lives inside of us. No matter what problems we are faced with, the entire Holy Trinity is right there on the scene, ready, willing and able to help us to the exact degree of our faith in the availability of this help. *"...I will be with him in trouble, I will deliver him and honor him"* (Psalm 91:15, *AMP*).

We are children of God. We never have to walk alone. He lives inside of us. He walks with us. Instead of struggling and straining, He wants us to relax and let Him be God. *"...God said, I will dwell in and with and among them and will walk in and with and among them, and I will be their God, and they shall be My people"* (II Corinthians 6:16, *AMP*).

The Holy Spirit is a tremendous source of strength. When we are at the end of our strength and can't go any further, His strength, power and might are fully available to us. *"...you shall receive power — ability, efficiency and might — when the Holy Spirit has come upon you"* (Acts 1:8, *AMP*).

We all need a guide when we go through difficult times. The more we study and meditate in God's Word, the more the Holy Spirit will guide us. He can see every twist and turn in the road ahead of us. He is able to guide us every step of the way during our lives here on earth. *"...He will be our guide even until death"* (Psalm 48:14, *AMP*).

He will bring us along the roads of life when we can't even begin to see the way. When the going is extremely difficult, He will smooth things out. He is always available to guide us and help us. *"I will lead the blind by ways they have not known, along unfamiliar paths I will guide them; I will turn the darkness into light before them and make the rough places smooth. These are the things I will do; I will not forsake them"* (Isaiah 42:16, *NIV*).

Birds know when it's time to go south and when it's time to fly north because of an inward leading that tells them when it's time to go and how to get where they are going. If God will guide birds, He certainly will guide us if we'll just seek His guidance continually instead of plunging on ahead, trying to figure everything out for ourselves.

When we don't know which way to turn, the Holy Spirit knows exactly where to turn. Every problem has an answer and the Holy Spirit has the answer to every problem. There is no such thing as an unsolvable problem for Him. We should continually turn to Him for guidance. "...the Lord will *continually guide you...*" (Isaiah 58:11, *NASV*).

God wants us walking by faith, not by sight. This is why He doesn't get out in front and show us exactly what to do. Instead, He wants us to learn what His Word says and then step out in faith on it. When we do this, we'll hear a still, small voice telling us exactly what road to take and when to turn to the right or to the left. "*And thine ears shall hear a word behind thee, saying, This is the way, walk ye in it, when ye turn to the right hand, and when ye turn to the left*" (Isaiah 30:21, *KJV*).

The Holy Spirit has every answer to every problem any of us will ever face. However, we can't hear His still, small voice unless we know how to "tune in" to it. The voices of Satan and his evil spirits are easy to hear. Satan is the god of this world (II Corinthians 4:4) and he speaks clearly to everyone, including God's children. However, the ability to "tune in" to the voice of the Holy Spirit must be *cultivated*. This does not come naturally. It comes a little at a time as we draw closer and closer to Him through daily study and meditation in His Word and daily worship, prayer and fellowship.

The Holy Spirit has immense spiritual power. "The Lord thy God in the midst of thee is *mighty*..." (Zephaniah 3:17, KJV). We need to stay close to Him through daily study, meditation, worship, prayer and fellowship. If we do these things continually, His power will be activated in our lives. If we don't, we block the flow of His power to us.

His power is so great that He was able to raise Jesus from the dead. This *same* magnificent power lives inside of us. "...the Spirit of God, who raised up Jesus from the dead, *lives in you*..." (Romans 8:11, TLB). What a waste it is to allow His Great Power to lie dormant if we don't know how it can be released in us and through us!

The power of the Holy Spirit is released *when we get into His will and stay in His will*. If we turn from His will towards our will, this *cuts off* the flow of His power. We release this power by continually studying the Word of God to learn God's will for our lives and then by obeying the instructions that we are given.

The Holy Spirit is the Author of God's Word. As we study and meditate continually in His Word, this opens the channel for the Author living in our hearts to speak directly to us. What a thrill it is to hear from the Holy Spirit each day...from His Book and also from His still, small voice continually speaking to us.

Satan tries to "jam" our minds with every possible distraction so that we can't hear the Holy Spirit speaking to us. He wants us to be so busy doing what we think is important that we think we can't find time to be alone with the Lord each day. We don't find time for this — we *make time*.

Our time with the Lord each day should be the

center of our lives. I wouldn't think of not spending at least 10% of the time that He has given me to be alone with Him any more than I would think of not giving at least 10% of the money that He has given me back to Him. There is no difference in the spiritual realm between time, money or any other gifts from God. If we want to receive from Him, we need to give freely from what He has given us. This is His law.

The Holy Spirit is always with us and He will help us and strengthen us. "Fear thou *not*; for *I am with thee*: be *not* dismayed; for I *am* thy God: I will strengthen thee; yea, I *will* help thee; yea, I *will* uphold thee with the right hand of my righteousness" (Isaiah 41:10, *KJV*).

No matter what we are going through, we can depend upon "...the God of all comfort, who comforts us in *all* our troubles..." (II Corinthians 1:3-4, *NIV*). He will comfort us just like a mother comforts a little child. "As one whom his mother comforteth, *so will I comfort you*..."(Isaiah 66:13, *KJV*). When we're so low that we think we're going to sink, He is there to comfort us and lift us up. "...God, Who *comforts* and *encourages* and *refreshes* and *cheers* the *depressed* and the *sinking*..." (II Corinthians 7:6, *AMP*).

It's important to realize that, when Jesus left the earth, He asked His Father to send the Holy Spirit to come to us. Jesus referred to the Holy Spirit as a "Comforter." "...I will ask the Father, and He will give you another *Comforter* (Counselor, Helper, Intercessor, Advocate, Strengthener and Standby) that He may *remain with you forever*..." (John 14:16, *AMP*).

What a joy it is to realize all of these promises from God's Word! All Christians will experience comfort when we get to heaven. This same comfort is available here on earth, but it isn't "automatic." If it was, there wouldn't be any troubled Christians here on earth and we know that this isn't true. In order to receive the comfort and all of the other benefits of the Holy Spirit, we must receive these benefits the way that we receive everything else from God in this earthly realm—*by faith.*

Our Father has unlimited strength and power and He shares this with us through the Holy Spirit. "...Out of his glorious, unlimited resources he will give you *the mighty inner strengthening of his Holy Spirit*" (Ephesians 3:16, *TLB*). When we are too weak to go any further, His strength is available to carry us the rest of the way. "...the (Holy) Spirit comes to our aid and *bears us up in our weakness...*" (Romans 8:26, *AMP*).

Our Father *never* promised us an easy life, but He *did* promise to be with us in every trial and to bring us through (if our faith is strong and enduring). "...*I will be with him in trouble, I will deliver him and honor him...*" (Psalm 91:15, *AMP*). No matter what we're going through, He is right there in the middle of the problem with us. "When thou passest through the waters, *I will be with thee*; and through the rivers, they shall *not* overflow thee: when thou walkest through the fire, thou shalt *not* be burned; *neither* shall the flame kindle upon thee" (Isaiah 43:2, *KJV*).

God never says, "Come back some other time when I'm not so busy." He is *always* available to us. The greatest Advisor this world has ever known is always there, just waiting for us to turn to Him. He is our constant Companion. When everything is falling apart He is there to help us. "The Lord is *close* to the brokenhearted and *saves* those who are crushed in spirit" (Psalm 34:18, *NIV*).

He is completely dependable. He will never let us down. "...*I will be with you; I will not fail you or forsake you*" (Joshua 1:5, *AMP*). No matter what we're going through, He will never leave us. "...*I will never leave thee, nor forsake thee*" (Hebrews 13:5, *KJV*). Christians will always be with Him — every minute of the rest of our lives here on earth and, after that, throughout eternity. "...*we shall always be with the Lord*" (I Thessalonians 4:17, *NASV*).

If we can even begin to comprehend the magnificence of the One who is always with us, we will never be afraid. "...*Be strong, vigorous and very courageous; be not afraid, neither be dismayed; for the Lord your God is with you wherever you go*" (Joshua 1:9, *AMP*).

Chapter 18
The Fullness Of The Holy Spirit

No matter what problem confronts us, the answer is available. The Holy Spirit has the answer to all problems. There is no problem that He cannot solve. He has never seen any problem that is too big for Him to handle.

The same God who created the Grand Canyon, Niagara Falls and all of the other wonders of this world lives inside of us. He decided how many million stars there would be and gave each of them a name. There is nothing that He cannot do. "He determines the number of the stars and calls them each by name. *Great* is our Lord and *mighty* in power; his understanding has *no limit*" (Psalm 147:4-5, *NIV*).

He assures us that we are the children of Almighty God. "The Spirit Himself [thus] testifies together with our own spirit, [assuring us] that *we are children of God*" (Romans 8:16, *AMP*). Because we are children of Almighty God, we have privileges in the spiritual realm that are reserved for members of the royal family. *Because* we are God's children, the Holy Spirit living inside of us is greater than *any* problem that Satan and his legions of fallen angels can bring against us. "*Ye are of God, little children, and have overcome them: because greater is he that is in you, than he that is in the world*" (I John 4:4, *KJV*).

If we will set aside time each day to draw closer to the Holy Spirit, He will open our eyes to great truths in the spiritual realm that we never knew existed. "...God has unveiled and revealed them by and through His Spirit, for the (Holy) Spirit searches diligently, exploring and examining everything, even sounding the profound and bottomless things of God — the divine counsels and things hidden and beyond man's scrutiny" (I Corinthians 2:10, *AMP*).

When we are faced with a very difficult situation and we have to open our mouths and come up with the proper answer, we shouldn't be concerned. If we open our mouths in faith, He will give us the words of wisdom that we need. "Now therefore go, and I *will* be with thy mouth, and *teach thee* what thou shalt say" (Exodus 4:12, *KJV*).

He doesn't want us to worry about what we're going to say. If we trust Him, He will give us the right words when we need them. "...do *not* be anxious about how or what you are to speak; for what you are to say *will be given you* in that very hour and moment" (Matthew 10:19, *AMP*). If we really trust Him, He will give us words and wisdom that are *so great* that our opponents will not be able to respond. "...I *will* give you words and wisdom that *none* of your adversaries will be able to resist or contradict" (Luke 21:15, *NIV*).

In these past two chapters we have seen several wonderful promises concerning the Holy Spirit. It's very easy to be enthusiastic about them and we should be enthusiastic. The word "enthusiasm" comes from two Greek words "en" and "theos." "En" means "in" and "theos" (from which we get the word "theological") means "God." **Enthusiasm actually means "God within us."**

When we meekly and humbly seek God's will each day of our lives, this puts us in position to receive the power of the Holy Spirit. When a jet airplane gets in the "jet stream" — a strong current of wind at a high altitude — it increases the speed of the airplane. We have a "jet stream" inside of us: the power of the Holy

Spirit. When we allow Him to control our lives, *then* His power will be released in us and through us.

Many of us sincerely want to do God's will, but something inside of us always seems to be pulling us in the other direction. That "something" is the carnal nature that we inherited from Adam. Before the Holy Spirit can work effectively in our lives, we have to bring our lower nature under the control of the new nature that we received from Jesus Christ when we were reborn spiritually:

"...*obey only the Holy Spirit's instructions.* He *will* tell you where to go and what to do, and then you won't always be doing the wrong things your evil nature wants you to. For we naturally love to do evil things that are just the opposite from the things that the Holy Spirit tells us to do; and the good things we want to do when the Spirit has his way with us are *just the opposite* of our natural desires. These two forces within us are constantly fighting each other to win control over us, and our wishes are never free from their pressures" (Galatians 5:16-17, *TLB*).

Jesus Christ surrendered His life for us. Now we must surrender our lives to Him. In order to be free, we need to give up our carnal, selfish desires and, instead, trust completely in Jesus Christ living within us to live His great life through us. "*I have been crucified with Christ* — in Him I have *shared His crucifixion*; it is *no longer I who live*, but *Christ, the Messiah, lives in me*; and the life I now live in the body *I live by faith* — by adherence to and reliance on and [complete] trust — in the Son of God, Who loved me and gave Himself up for me" (Galatians 2:20, *AMP*).

Human efforts do not produce results in the spiritual realm. *Spiritual results are produced through us, not by us.* Spiritual results come when we yield to the Holy Spirit and trust in Him. When we do these two things each day of our lives, this opens up the channel through which His power will flow.

No matter what problems we come up against, *if* we surrender them to the Holy Spirit and *if* we trust in Him, He will help us to solve them. "...*by our faith* the Holy Spirit *helps us* with our daily problems..." (Romans 8:26, *TLB*).

Jesus Christ wants to make His permanent home on earth in our hearts. "May Christ through your faith [actually] dwell — settle down, abide, make His permanent home — in your hearts!..." (Ephesians 3:17, *AMP*). He will live in our hearts *in proportion to our faith*.

The key to releasing the power of the living Christ — the Holy Spirit living within us — is to *know how to be filled* with the Holy Spirit. God's Word tells us that He *wants us* to be filled with the Spirit. "...*be filled* (through *all* your being) unto *all* the fullness of God..." (Ephesians 3:19, *AMP*). "...ever be *filled* and stimulated with the (Holy) Spirit" (Ephesians 5:18, *AMP*).

What does it mean to be filled with the Spirit? It means that the Holy Spirit should fill every area of our lives, every day of our lives. Everything that we think, say or do should revolve around our consciousness of His magnificent indwelling presence. A continual consciousness of His presence and His ability will always strengthen us and bring us through whatever comes against us.

Many people search for worldly security, but the truth is that the Holy Spirit living within us is the greatest security that we can have. When the going is really tough and we can't see any way out, the greatest asset that we can have is a deep inner certainty of Who lives inside of us and what He can and will do in us and through us if our faith is strong enough to let go and trust Him completely.

How do we go about being filled with the Holy Spirit? **We are filled with the Spirit to the degree that we live our lives as if they are not our own.** In order to be Spirit-filled, we need to willingly and cheerfully surrender our God-given right to live as we want to live and voluntarily yield to the Holy Spirit, continually seeking His will for our lives.

How do we do this? I believe that this starts the first thing every morning if we start our day by opening our mouths and, speaking from the heart, relinquish control of the day ahead and ask Him to reveal His will and to guide us in His will throughout the coming day. This continues by surrendering continually to Him throughout each day.

It is very important to do this on a *daily* basis. "...If any person wills to come after Me, let him *deny himself* — that is, disown himself, forget, lose sight of himself and his own interests, refuse and give up himself — and take up his cross *daily*, and follow Me..." (Luke 9:23, *AMP*).

This is the key to the Spirit-filled life — to give up our personal desires and to surrender to the Holy Spirit all day long, each and every day of our lives. *All of us are as full of the Spirit as we really want to be.* Far too many of us aren't filled with the Spirit because we don't get precious time alone with Him each day and because we don't willingly surrender to Him throughout each day because we are spending far too much time doing what *we* want to do.

He will never force Himself on us. Evil spirits try to do this, but the Holy Spirit doesn't. He waits for us to give up our free will and willingly turn to Him. Sadly, many of us do this very little, if at all, and *thereby deny ourselves the greatest power in the entire world.*

Being filled with the Spirit is a *continuous* process, not a one-time occurrence. Almost every day we are involved with problems — our own and those of other people. As we deal with these daily problems, we pour out emotional energy. We need to be "refilled" every day to restore what we lose each day.

As we turn each day to the Holy Spirit over a period of weeks, months and years, He will reveal more and more of His will to us and give us more and more of the spiritual understanding that we will require in order to deal with the challenges and problems that we will face. "...be *filled* with the full (deep and clear) knowledge of *His will* in all spiritual wisdom [that is, in comprehensive insight into the ways and purposes of God] and in *understanding* and *discernment* of spiritual things..." (Colossians 1:9, *AMP*).

No matter how bad our problems might be, if we turn continually to the Lord, He will fill us with His hope, joy and peace to the degree that we trust Him. "May the God of your hope *so fill you* with all joy and peace in believing — through the experience of your faith — that by the power of the Holy Spirit you may *abound and be overflowing (bubbling over) with hope...*" (Romans 15:13, *AMP*).

When we're going through painful, difficult times, God's Word tells us exactly what to do. "...it was too great an effort for me and too painful, *until* I went into the sanctuary of God..." (Psalm 73:16-17, *AMP*). A sanctuary is a place where we can go for rest and refreshment. Our Father has provided us with such a sanctuary deep down inside of our hearts. This is where the Holy Spirit lives. Satan can only get at us when we come out of the sanctuary that God has provided for us and focus in on the problems that he is trying to give us instead of focusing completely on the calm, quiet, totally victorious Holy Spirit living within us.

The greatest asset that any of us will ever have is the fullness that comes from a close, continuing trust in and submission to Almighty God Himself living in our hearts. This relationship will enable us to emerge victorious over any and all problems that any of us will ever experience.

"Grace is receiving what we do not deserve; mercy is not receiving what we do deserve."

Chapter 19
The Grace Of God

In the previous eighteen chapters of this book, I have given the reader hundreds of verses of Scripture to explain exactly what our heavenly Father wants us to do when we are faced with difficult problems. However, what happens to Christians who are faced with difficult problems and are *unable* to follow all of these instructions? Is everything lost? Is failure inevitable? No, everything isn't lost and failure isn't inevitable.

When we do our best to follow these instructions but don't stick to them, our heavenly Father does make allowances for us to get up again, brush ourselves off and start anew. When we miss the mark, we can always go to our Father and repent and ask Him to have mercy upon us.

Our heavenly Father knows our hearts. He knows exactly how much we are able to do. He knows just how much we can stand. He knows how strong our faith is. He takes all of these and many other variables into consideration. In His wisdom, He makes *grace* available to us when we can't go any further.

The word "grace" comes from the Greek word "charis" which means a gift that is undeserved. Everything in the Old Testament was under the law. Everything in the New Testament is by grace. In the Old Testament the people earned everything. In the New Testament we are given gifts from God that *we have not earned.*

Our Lord Jesus Christ is the channel of God's grace. When we go to our heavenly Father in the name of the Lord Jesus Christ, He will give us grace, not because of anything that we did to deserve it, but because of the price that Jesus Christ paid for us.

Jesus paid the price for all of our sins and this opened the door for our heavenly Father to give us many wonderful gifts that we have not earned. "For out of His fullness (abundance) we all received — all had a share and we were all supplied with — one grace after another and spiritual blessing upon spiritual blessing, and even favor upon favor and gift [heaped] upon gift. For while the Law was given through Moses, *grace — unearned, undeserved favor and spiritual blessing — and truth came through Jesus Christ*" (John 1:16-17, *AMP*).

When a Christian is reborn spiritually, this occurrence takes place by the grace of God. All of us are sinners and none of us could possibly earn our salvation. This is a gift of God paid for by Jesus Christ. "...*all* have sinned and are falling short of the honor and glory which God bestows and receives. [*All*] are justified and made upright and in right standing with God, freely and gratuitously *by His grace* (His unmerited favor and mercy), through the redemption which is [provided] in Christ Jesus..." (Romans 3:23-24, *AMP*).

Because of the sin of Adam, the entire human race is under the penalty of death. Because Jesus paid for Adam's sins, God's wonderful grace allows every human being to receive the free gift of eternal salvation. "For if, because of one man's trespass (lapse, offense) death reigned through that one, much more surely will those who receive [*God's*] *overflowing grace* (unmerited favor) and the free gift of righteousness (putting them into right standing with Himself)

150

reign as kings in life through the One, Jesus Christ, the Messiah, the Anointed One" (Romans 5:17, *AMP*).

That *same* wonderful grace that is available to each of us in order to receive salvation is *also* available to us as we go through trials and tribulations in our lives. When we do our best and still fail, we *can* turn to our heavenly Father and ask Him for His grace that we don't earn, deserve or merit. This grace — this undeserved kindness — is available to us because of His love, kindness and compassion. "The Lord's lovingkindnesses indeed never cease, for His compassions never fail. They are new every morning; great is Thy faithfulness" (Lamentations 3:22-23, *NASV*).

His grace is available to us *because He loves us more than we can even begin to comprehend.* "...May your roots go down deep into the soil of God's marvelous love; and may you be able to feel and understand, as all God's children should, how long, how wide, how deep, and how high his love really is; and to experience this love for yourselves, though it is *so great* that you will *never* see the end of it or fully know or understand it..." (Ephesians 3:17-19, *TLB*).

Our Father wants us to do the very best that we can to follow all of the instructions from His Word that I have explained in the previous chapters. However, when we have done our best and we don't have the faintest idea where to go from there, this is the time to cry out to our Father and ask for His grace. Once we have done everything that we can, He wants us to let go, trusting completely in His mercy and His grace.

Grace is receiving what we do not deserve. Mercy is not receiving what we do deserve. In His wisdom, our Father decides when to reach out to us with mercy and compassion. His Word says, "...'I will have mercy on whom I have mercy, and I will have compassion on whom I have compassion.' It does *not*, therefore, depend on man's desire or effort, but on God's mercy" (Romans 9:15-16, *NIV*).

When we carefully follow the instructions that are explained in this book, our heavenly Father will do exactly what His Word says He will do. However, when we do our best and come up short, this *doesn't* mean that He won't bring us through. Our Father can do *whatever* He wants to do in His permissive will and many times His love and compassion release grace to us when we would fail completely without it.

One of the best ways to understand how our heavenly Father treats us when we are in a situation like this is to think how little children trust their human father when they are unable to do something. All of us have seen little children do the very best that they can and come up short and then turn to their father and ask him to take it from there. Our heavenly Father does the same thing. He says, "Be calm. Everything is going to be all right. You did your best. Trust Me to do the rest."

God's grace is available to us only to the degree that we come to Him in full admission of our weakness and humble ourselves before Him. In a previous chapter we looked at II Corinthians 12:9 in a different context. We saw that God's strength and power is made perfect when we admit our weakness. Now let's look at this again in relation to His grace. "...*My grace* — My favor and loving-kindness and mercy — are *enough* for you, [that is, sufficient against *any* danger and to enable you to bear the trouble manfully]; for My strength and power are made perfect — fulfilled and completed and show themselves most effective — in [your] weakness..." (II Corinthians 12:9, *AMP)*.

In order to receive the grace of God, it is best for us to openly admit our weakness. When we do this, this gives Him the channel that He needs to release his strength to be made perfect in our weakness. When we know that we don't have any way of solving the problem ourselves, our heavenly Father often comes through in the midst of this weakness.

When this happens, we know that He did it because we know that we were completely helpless. God's grace is seen in our insufficiency. When we know that we can't go any further and we admit it, we humble ourselves before Him. *This* is when we receive undeserved favors. "...He gives His undeserved favor to the low [in rank], the humble and the afflicted" (Proverbs 3:34, *AMP*).

God's grace is released to those with humble hearts. Humble hearts are grateful to the Lord. Humble hearts know how little we are and how magnificent the Lord is. Grace is *not* available to the proud, but it *is* available to the humble. "...He gives us more and more grace [power of the Holy Spirit, to meet this evil tendency and all others fully]. That is why He says, God sets Himself *against* the proud and haughty, but *gives grace* [continually] to the lowly — those who are humble-minded [enough to receive it]" (James 4:6, *AMP*).

God's grace is available to us when we openly admit our inadequacy. Many times when we have done our best, we then have to come to the Lord and throw ourselves on His mercy and ask for His grace. We need to come to Him stripped of all pride and arrogance, humbling ourselves completely before Him. Only with this humble attitude are we able to let go of our problems:

"...Clothe (apron) yourselves, all of you, with *humility* — as the garb of a servant, so that its covering cannot possibly be stripped from you, with freedom from pride and arrogance — toward one another. For God sets Himself *against* the proud — the insolent, the overbearing, the disdainful, the presumptuous, the boastful, and opposes, frustrates and defeats them — but *gives grace (favor, blessing) to the humble.* Therefore humble yourselves (demote, lower yourselves in your own estimation) under the mighty hand of God, that in due time He may exalt you. Casting the *whole* of your care — *all* your anxieties, *all* your worries, *all* your concerns, *once and for all* — on Him; for He cares for you affectionately, and cares about you watchfully" (I Peter 5:5-7, *AMP).*

The Lord Jesus Christ knows exactly what we are going through. No matter how painful our suffering is, it is not theoretical to him. He understands. He sympathizes with us. He knows *exactly* how much we are hurting because He has been through exactly what each of us is going through. Because He has been where we are and never failed, this enables us to come to the throne of God and ask Him to give us wonderful gifts that we do not merit:

"For we do *not* have a High Priest Who is *unable* to understand and sympathize and have a fellow feeling with our weaknesses and infirmities and liability to the assaults of temptation, but One Who *has* been tempted in *every* respect as we are, yet without sinning. Let us then fearlessly and confidently and boldly draw near to *the throne of grace* — the throne of God's unmerited favor [to us sinners]; that we may *receive mercy* [for our failures] and *find grace* to help in good time for every need — appropriate help and well-timed help, coming just when we need it" (Hebrews 4:15-16, *AMP).*

Sometimes we find ourselves in situations where we are hurting deeply because someone else has sinned against us. When this happens, we can be comforted in knowing that God's Word says that the *more* sin we are faced with, the *more* God's grace is available to us. "...where sin *increased* and *abounded,* grace (God's unmerited favor) has *surpassed* it and *increased* the more and *superabounded*" (Romans 5:20, *AMP).*

There is absolutely no limit to the amount of grace that our heavenly Father is able to make available to us. No matter what we need, His grace is completely sufficient. "And God is able to make *all grace (every* favor and earthly blessing) come to you *in abundance,* so that you may always and under all circumstances and *whatever* the need, be self-sufficient — possessing enough to require no aid or support and furnished in abundance for every good work and charitable donation" (II Corinthians 9:8, *AMP).*

So, we should do our very best to follow the instructions from God's Word that have been explained in this book. Once we have done our best, we then should place our complete trust in our heavenly Father's wonderful grace that is available to all of His children when we come to Him in admitted weakness, humbling ourselves before Him and trusting completely in Him.

*"We should use our 'summertime'—
the time when things are
going well in our lives—to gather
an abundant harvest of
spiritual truth and store it
up in our hearts for the
'winter' days that are sure to come."*

Conclusion

At the beginning of this book I promised you a detailed, step-by-step set of instructions showing exactly what God's Word says about how to deal with the trials and tribulations that all of us will face. Since then we have carefully examined hundreds of verses of Scripture on this subject.

We have seen why we have to go through adversity, how we can grow and mature through adversity and how our Father wants us to react to adversity. We have seen how God can solve problems that seem insolvable to us and why and how to focus on Him instead of our problems.

We have seen how the Lord's timing is different from ours and what it means to wait on the Lord. We have seen what God's Word has to say about the necessity for patience and endurance when we face adversity. We have taken a good look at Romans 8:28 to see what it really means.

We have discussed how praise, thanksgiving and rejoicing in the Lord is necessary during times of adversity. We have discussed the power of prayer, how to give our problems to the Lord and how to use God's strength instead of our own. We have discussed the magnificence of the Holy Spirit living in our hearts and what we need to do so that His power can be released in our lives. We have discussed the magnificent grace of God that is available to us.

Too many of us get in the midst of life's storms without a map or a guide. Our Father doesn't want us to do this. He has given us a map, His Word. He has given us a guide, the Holy Spirit. *Will we* use this map? *Will we* listen carefully to our Guide and follow His instructions?

Too many of us are complacent in our temporary well-being. Too many of us think, "All of this is good, but I don't need it. I'm getting along fine." *This is exactly how Satan wants us to think.* He wants us to feel happy and content in our own little world. With every year of this complacency that goes by, he knows that it is going to be that much easier for him when he finally "lowers the boom" on us.

Too many of us trust in our gifts (our abilities, our health, our finances, our families) instead of trusting in the Giver. Too many of us fail to prepare for the inevitable severe storms that all of us will face. God's Word is full of instructions. It is also full of promises. We need to learn and obey the instructions in order to receive the promises. They aren't "automatic." God provides a shelter for every storm, but we need to learn how to find that shelter and how to get into it.

Now is the time to build a solid spiritual foundation for all of the problems that all of us will face. "He that gathereth in summer is a wise son..." (Proverbs 10:5, *KJV)*. Summer is the time to gather in the crop and to store it up for the winter months ahead.

We should use our "summertime" — the time when things are going well in our lives — to gather an abundant harvest of spiritual truth and store it up in our hearts for the "winter" days that are sure to come. If we spend our time wisely when all is well, we'll be equipped to deal with the problems that all of us will face when all is not well.

Now is the time to start using these principles to trust the Lord for our small problems so that we will be able to deal with the big problems that are sure to come. If they don't come any other time, we can be sure that they will come when we are "senior citizens." Old age is always the harvest time when we reap what we have sown during preceding years.

This book is not just to "read." It must be "studied." Many people don't want to pay this price, but for those who do, let me offer some suggestions. Go back through this book and mark it up with a pen or a highlighter. Underline. Draw rectangles around parts that are important to you. Make notes in the margin. Take the test at the end of this book over and over until you can pass it with a high score.

Take the key verses of Scripture from this book and type or print them neatly on 3" x 5" cards. Take *one* card with you each day. Meditate on that verse of Scripture all day long. Turn it over and over in your mind, looking at it from every conceivable angle. Personalize it. Apply it to your own situation.

Open your mouth and speak this verse of Scripture over and over. Put it in the first person. Claim it for yourself. Thank the Lord again and again for it. Praise Him. When we open our mouths and speak God's Word (or words which line up with His Word), we release God's spiritual power.

Continue to meditate and speak this verse of Scripture until it drops from your mind down into your heart. Then, take your next 3" x 5" card and repeat the same process. Keep on doing this until you have repeated this process carefully on every card. Don't rush! Go as slowly as you need to go in order to plant each verse of Scripture in your heart.

It will take several months to do this project correctly. During this time you will continually be planting positive "seeds" in your heart. These seeds will take root and grow. Soon they will produce a harvest. You will be able to successfully overcome problems that seemed impossible in the past.

Be patient. This growth doesn't happen immediately. There is always a period of time between seedtime and harvest. However, while you're waiting, you'll be continually planting more and more seeds. As this process continues, you will *"know that you know that you know"* that you are on the right track This will keep you going until your harvest starts to come in.

If this process of meditating on Scripture, speaking it constantly with your mouth and doing exactly what it says to do is repeated over a period of time, you *will succeed* in overcoming the problem. Either that is true or God's Word is not true because it says, "This book of the law shall *not* depart from your mouth, but you shall *meditate* on it day and night, so that you may be careful to *do* according to all that is written in it; for then you *will* make your way prosperous, and then you *will* have success" (Joshua 1:8, *NASV)*.

This doesn't say that we "might" have success. It says that we *will* have success. This process of continual confession plus continual meditation plus doing exactly what God's Word says to do *will* produce results! This has happened *again* and *again* in my own life. I have seen these principles succeed *many, many* times with other people.

This process *will* work for you if you are willing to pay this price for a period of several months. This process will continue to work for you if you continue to pay this price for the rest of your life. What a glorious life this is when we follow the three principles of Joshua 1:8 every day of our lives!

It works beautifully. God will always do His part. Will we do ours? Will we pay this price day in and day out over a long period of time? Those of us who won't pay the price will ultimately pay a much harder price. Do it the right way. Do it God's way. Pay this price now and keep on paying it! **I guarantee you that this will transform your life.**

What Did You Learn From This Book?

One way of finding out how much you have retained from this book is to take the following test. How many answers do you know now — while this book is still fresh in your mind? I suggest that you mark your calendar to take this test again on a specific date — thirty to ninety days from now, to check your retention after a period of time.

This book will only help you to the degree that it can persuade you to change your habits to line up with the instructions that our Father has given us to follow if we want to learn how to soar above the problems of life.

Question	*Page Ref.
1. Why is it important for us to learn God's ways of solving problems instead of trying to solve problems the same way that the world does?	7
2. Many of us have to deal with problems that are beyond human comprehension. Will we ever understand why we had to go through these problems?	9
3. Who led Jesus Christ into a period of trials and temptation at the start of His earthly ministry?	9
4. Most of us take a daily bath or shower to cleanse our bodies. How do we cleanse our souls?	10
5. If we refuse to study and meditate continually in the Word of God, what other method does our heavenly Father use to cleanse us?	11

*"God wants us to come
to Him,
not as intellectuals,
but as little children."*

Appendix

Have You Entered
Into The Kingdom Of God?

You have just read a complete summary of God's Word pertaining to the subject of adversity. These are laws that our Father has written for His children—those human beings who have entered into His kingdom. I ask each reader of this book, "Have *you* entered into the kingdom of God?"

Jesus Christ said, "...Verily, verily, I say unto thee, Except a man be born again, he cannot see the kingdom of God" (John 3:3). Jesus went on to say, "...Ye must be born again" (John 3:7). It is very clear that there is only one way to enter into the kingdom of God and that is to be "born again."

We don't enter into God's kingdom by church attendance, by teaching Sunday School, by baptism, by confirmation or by living a good life. Jesus Christ paid the price for every one of us to enter into God's kingdom, but this is not "automatic." Many people are so caught up with their own religious denomination or their own personal beliefs that they completely miss God's specific instructions as to how to enter into His kingdom—for the rest of our lives on earth and also for eternity in heaven.

In order to become a born-again Christian, we first of all, must admit that we are sinners (Romans 3:23, James 2:10). We must admit that there is absolutely no way that we can enter into God's kingdom based upon our own merits. Next, we have to genuinely repent of our sins (Luke 13:3, Acts 3:19).

After this admission of sin and repentance there is one additional step that must be taken in order to become a born-again Christian. "For if you *tell others* with your own mouth that Jesus Christ is your Lord, and *believe* in your own heart that God has raised Him from the dead, you *will* be saved. For it is by believing in his *heart* that a man becomes right with God; and with his *mouth* he tells others of his faith, confirming his salvation" (Romans 10:9-10, *TLB*).

Many people know that Jesus Christ died for our sins. However, knowledge isn't enough. Intellectual agreement isn't enough. In order to be born again, we have to accept Jesus as our Saviour in our *hearts* and not just in our heads. We're not born again until we come to Him as admitted sinners and trust Him deep down in our hearts as the only way that we can enter into the kingdom of God. God knows exactly what we believe deep down in our hearts (I Samuel 16:7, I Chronicles 28:9, Hebrews 4:13).

We must believe in our hearts that Jesus Christ is the Son of God, that He was born of a virgin, that He died on the cross to pay for our sins, that He rose again from the dead and that He lives today. In order to be a born-again Christian, Romans 10:9-10 tells us that we must not only believe this in our hearts, but we *also* must open our *mouths* and tell others of this belief. This confirms our salvation.

When you believe this in your heart and tell others of this belief with your mouth, *then* you are a born-again Christian. All of us were born naturally on the day that our mothers gave birth to us. We must have a second birth—a spiritual birth—in order to enter into God's kingdom. "For you have a new life. It was not passed on to you from your parents, for the life they gave you will fade away. This new one will last forever, for it comes from Christ, God's ever-living Message to men" (I Peter 1:23, *TLB).*

God wants us to come to Him, not as intellectuals, but as little children. God doesn't reveal Himself to us through our intellects. He reveals Himself to us through our hearts and, in order to enter into His kingdom, we must come to Him as little children. We may be adults in the natural world, but in the spiritual world we have to start all over. We have to be born again as spiritual babies. Jesus said, "...Except ye be converted, and become as little children, ye shall not enter into the kingdom of heaven" (Matthew 18:3, *KJV).*

The following prayer will cause you to become born again if you believe this in your heart and open your mouth and tell others of this belief:

"Dear Father, I come to You in the Name of Jesus Christ. I admit that I am a sinner and I know there is no way that I can enter into Your kingdom based upon the sinful life that I have led. I'm genuinely sorry for my sins and I ask for Your mercy. I believe in my heart that Jesus Christ is Your Son—that He was born of a virgin, that He died on the cross to pay for my sins, that You raised Him from the dead and that He is alive today. I trust in Him as my only way of entering into Your kingdom. I confess now to You, Father, that Jesus Christ is my Saviour and my Lord and I will tell others of this decision now and in the future. Thank You, Father. Amen."

When you believe this in your heart and confess this to others with your mouth, you have been reborn spiritually. You are brand new in the spiritual realm.

"Therefore if any man be in Christ, he is a *new* creature: old things are *passed away;* behold, *all* things are become new" (II Corinthians 5:17, *KJV).*

Now that you have a new, recreated spirit, you are ready to study, understand and obey God's laws pertaining to adversity and all of His other laws. This will transform the rest of your life on earth and you also will live forever in heaven. "For God so loved the world, that he gave his only begotten Son, that whosoever believeth in him should not perish, but have everlasting life" (John 3:16, *KJV).*

A Request To Our Readers

Has this book helped you? If so, would you be willing to tell others so that this book can help them too? Many people are naturally skeptical about the advertising claims for a book such as this. This is why we use a large number of "testimonials" from satisfied readers in our advertising for this book.

If this book has helped you, I'd appreciate it if you would write to me in care of the publisher. Please tell me in your own words how this book has helped you and why you would recommend it to others. Please give us as much information as you can.

Also, we will need your written permission to use any part or all of your comments, your name and the town or city that you live in (we never use street addresses) for our advertising for this book.

Thank you for helping us and, most important, for helping others.

Jack Hartman
Lamplight Publications
P.O. Box 3293
Manchester, NH 03105

Other Books by Jack Hartman

Jack Hartman is a self-employed businessman. In 1974, he was on the verge of bankruptcy and a nervous breakdown. He was almost paralyzed by worry and fear. At that time he accepted Jesus Christ as Saviour and Lord.

He immediately started to study and meditate day and night in the Holy Scriptures to learn how to solve his financial and emotional problems. After several months of study he was able to apply these Biblical principles to his problems and they worked!

His business has turned completely around, all debts have been paid off right on schedule and his business has grown steadily each year since then. In addition, he and three other businessmen started a Bible study class in his office which now has grown into a large church with average Sunday morning attendance of 1,000 people.

The growth of this business and the growth of this church have come as a result of applying Biblical principles which Jack has explained in his book *Trust God For Your Finances.*

The principles in this book are not theoretical. They have worked in Jack Hartman's life and in the lives of many people who have counseled with him. Now these principles are available in book form.

Jack carefully points out the differences between the world's system of prosperity and God's laws of prosperity. He explains that all of the warnings in the Bible against financial prosperity are warnings against following the *world's* system of prosperity.

Our Father very *definitely* wants His children to prosper as long as they follow His laws of prosperity. These laws are laid out in detail in sixteen chapters of specific instruction—every chapter filled with many verses of Scripture.

Trust God For Your Finances can be ordered for $4.95 per copy plus 10% postage and handling. The order form for this is at the end of this book.

As a Bible study teacher and a Christian counselor, Jack has encountered many worried, anxious and fearful people over the years. They worry about family problems... health problems...employment problems...The list goes on and on.

However, our Lord Jesus told us not to be worried, troubled or afraid. He wouldn't have told us this if it were impossible to do.

Despite the adversity He faced, Jesus didn't worry. Although He has given this same peace to us to sustain us during our trials and tribulations, receiving this peace is not "automatic". It is actually similar to money in a bank account. Jesus made the "deposit" of peace for us, but we have to learn to make "withdrawals".

Deep Inner Peace is an in-depth study of what the Bible has to say about God-given peace. The principles in this book are not theoretical. They have worked successfully in Jack Hartman's life and in the lives of many people who have followed these principles.

Jack carefully points out the differences between the world's ideas of peace and the *deep inner peace* that comes from knowing Christ, the Prince of peace. He believes that God's Word clearly sets forth the formula for true, lasting peace. These principles are laid out in detail in eighteen chapters of scriptural truth. The book closes with a unique "test" in which readers may test themselves on their knowledge of God's *deep inner peace*. It is the author's sincere belief that you can never be the same after reading this book and giving yourself this test.

Deep Inner Peace can be ordered for $4.95 per copy plus 10% postage and handling. Use the order form at the end of this book.

Jack Hartman

As soon as Jack accepted Christ as his personal Saviour, he began an intensive study of God's Word. From the very first day of this study and meditation the Lord led him to write "Spiritual Meditations" on the spiritual truths that he learned that day. He now has written over 60,000 (!) of these meditations and he continues to write them almost every day of his life.

Jack has now written a book of his best spiritual meditations on the subject of faith. The title of this book is *Nuggets of Faith*. There are over eighty of these "nuggets" (average length—3 paragraphs) which are the result of thousands of hours of research and study.

There are no wasted words in this book. Each of these "nuggets" goes straight to the point. This book will give you maximum results in a minimum of time. It will make you think.

You can easily read this book in one day. On the other hand, each of these "nuggets" contains enough depth so that you can take one "nugget" with you in the morning and dwell on it throughout the day, turning its scriptural truth over and over in your mind as you meditate on how this scriptural truth can apply to your life.

Nuggets of Faith can be ordered for $2.50 per copy plus 10% postage and handling. The order form for this is at the end of this book.

100 YEARS FROM TODAY

Jack Hartman

In his early years as a Bible study teacher, Jack Hartman saw the necessity of an easy-to-read book that unsaved people could read, showing them their need for salvation. As a result, *One Hundred Years From Today* was written in Bible study form and was made available to those who attended Jack's Bible study classes. Now it has been revised and printed as a book and is available to all of Jack's readers.

One Hundred Years From Today is the perfect witnessing tool. After pointing out that every word in the Bible is inspired by God Himself, Jack goes on to explain what salvation is...why we must be saved...how to become saved...where we will be one hundred years from today if we are saved—and if we are not.

This book uses simple language to clearly show that there are two roads that can be taken and that we must make our decision while we're alive on this earth. Jack warns the reader not to trust in religion or in good works in order to get to heaven. He makes it very clear that *Jesus is the only way.*

The reason for the effectiveness of this scripture-packed study is Jack's conversational style. He spares the complex theological language, gets right to the point and makes an appeal to the reader to pray a sinner's prayer. You can be assured that, upon finishing this book, the reader will have been told the message of salvation through Jesus Christ.

Hundreds of people have come to know Jesus as a result of reading *One Hundred Years From Today* when it was in Bible study form, and many more will receive Jesus as Lord and Saviour now that it has been published. *One Hundred Years From Today* can be ordered for $2.95 per copy plus 10% postage and handling. The order form for this is at the end of this book.

HOW TO STUDY THE BIBLE

At last — a proven, effective method for studying God's Word.

Jack Hartman

One thing that is obvious about Jack Hartman is his deep love for the Word of God. Ever since his close brush with personal bankruptcy and a nervous breakdown, he has devoted his life to the study of the Scriptures. Nothing is more exciting to Jack than to receive fresh, new truths from God's Word.

How To Study The Bible explains the specific method that Jack uses to study God's Word. It has worked successfully for him and the students in his Bible study classes. Many letters have been received from all over the world commenting on the effectiveness of this method of Bible study.

The importance of studying God's Word is made clear in the Scriptures. Not only does Jack show why God says we must study His Word—he also gives definite, step-by-step instructions for the method he uses.

Jack has found that many people try to study God's Word, only to give up after a while, confused and frustrated. *How To Study The Bible* carefully explains a proven, effective method that will help any reader to learn how to solve specific problems in his or her life.

Jack's system of Bible study is easy to understand, but involves a lot of hard work and discipline. However, the rewards of studying God's Word make it well worth the effort.

How To Study The Bible can be ordered for $3.50 per copy plus 10% postage and handling. The order form for this is at the end of this book.

Would you risk your life to get a copy of the Bible? Most of us have never had to answer this question, but it must be answered daily by Christians who live behind the Iron Curtain. In these countries, the Bible is considered harmful to the Communist system and ownership can cause very serious trouble.

Mission: Possible tells the story of one man's ministry to the persecuted Church behind the Iron Curtain. This book is filled with miracles of God as Hans Kristian smuggled Bibles into Communist countries. In addition to telling of these dangerous adventures, it also shows us a side of Christianity that we in the "free world" rarely have the opportunity to see.

Hans Kristian tells the story of the risk that these believers take to obey God. They risk being arrested... losing their jobs...their children...even their lives. They must count the cost each time they leave their homes to attend a Christian meeting because they may never return.

Many readers will find themselves asking the same questions that Hans Kristian asked when he first started his ministry to believers behind the Iron Curtain: "If this was Christianity, then what was the game we were playing in the West?"

Hans Kristian's missionary work to Communist countries is now in its twenty-second year. This amazing book has sold 840,000 copies and has been translated in 25 languages. It can be ordered for $3.50 per copy plus 10% postage and handling. The order form for this is at the end of this book.

Cassette Tapes
By Jack Hartman

Tape #   **Title**

01H **How To Study The Bible (Part I)**—21 scriptural reasons why it is so important to study the Bible.

02H **How To Study The Bible (Part II)**—a step-by-step detailed explanation of a proven effective system for studying the Bible (our most demanded tape).

03H **Enter Into God's Rest**—Don't struggle and strain with loads that are too heavy for you. Learn exactly what God's Word teaches about relaxing under pressure.

04H **Freedom From Worry**—a comprehensive scriptural explanation on how to become completely free from worry.

05H **God's Strength—Our Weakness**—God's strength is available to the degree that we can admit our human weakness and trust, instead, in His unlimited strength.

06H **How To Transform Our Lives**—a thorough, scriptural study of how we can change our lives completely through a complete spiritual renewal of our minds.

07H **The Greatest Power In The Universe (Part I)**—the greatest power in the universe is love. Part I gives a beautiful scriptural explanation of our Father's love for us.

08H **The Greatest Power In The Universe (Part II)**—a thorough scriptural explanation on our love for God, our love for each other and overcoming fear through love.

09H **How Well Do You Know Jesus Christ?**—an Easter Sunday message that received great audience response. After this message, you'll know Jesus Christ as you never knew Him before.

10H **God's Perfect Peace**—In a world of unrest, people everywhere are searching for inner peace. This is a detailed scriptural explanation of how to obtain God's perfect peace.

11H **Freedom Through Surrender**—Millions of people are trying to find freedom by "doing their own thing." God's Word tells us to do just the opposite. Freedom comes only as a result of daily surrender of our lives to Jesus Christ.

12H **Overcoming Anger**—Do you know when anger is permissible and when it is a sin? Learn step-by-step procedures from the Bible on how to overcome the sinful effects of anger.

13H **Taking Possession Of Our Souls**—God's Word teaches that patience is the key to the possession of our souls. Learn why God allows us to have severe problems, why He sometimes makes us wait for His answer and how to increase patience and endurance.

14H **Staying Young In The Lord**—Our generation tries to cover up the aging process with makeup, hair coloring, hairpieces, etc. The Bible teaches us a better way. Learn specific factual methods to offset the aging process.

15H **Two Different Worlds**—A specific explanation of how to enter into the spiritual realm in order to learn the great truths that our Father wants to reveal to us.

16H **Trust God For Your Finances**—We have had many requests for a cassette tape of Jack Hartman's book "Trust God For Your Finances." In response to this request, this tape was made and it contains a summary of the highlights of the book.

17H ***The Joy of the Lord**—What is the difference between pleasure, happiness and joy? How can Christians experience the joy of the Lord regardless of external circumstances that they are faced with? This message carefully examines over forty scriptural references and carefully details seventeen different Biblical requirements for receiving the joy of the Lord.

18H ***Let Go and Let God**—Most Christians know that the Word of God tells us to let go of our problems and give them to God. However, many of us find that this is easier to say than it is to do. Find out how to let go of your problems and how to leave them with the Lord instead of taking them back.

19H ***Guidance, Power, Comfort and Wisdom**—In this tape Jack tells how the Holy Trinity lives inside each believer, and why it is essential for us to experience the Divine Presence of God. The message reveals that the greatest Power in the universe can guide, comfort in trouble and bring to us the bottomless truth of God. The tape ends with instructions on releasing this guidance, power, comfort and wisdom in your life.

*These cassette tapes are new...since Jack's last book, *How To Study The Bible* was published.

Book/Cassette Tape Order Form

To order books and cassette tapes by Jack Hartman, please use this order form:

Books	Qty.	Price
Trust God For Your Finances ($4.95)	_____	$ _____
Nuggets Of Faith ($2.50)	_____	$ _____
Deep Inner Peace ($4.95)	_____	$ _____
How To Study The Bible ($3.50)	_____	$ _____
100 Years From Today ($2.95)	_____	$ _____
Mission Possible ($3.50)	_____	$ _____
Soaring Above The Problems Of Life ($5.95)	_____	$ _____

Cassette Tapes $4.00 ea.
(or $3.00 ea. if three or more tapes are ordered).
Check the tapes that you wish to order.

__ 01H __ 02H __ 03H __ 04H __ 05H __ 06H
__ 07H __ 08H __ 09H __ 10H __ 11H __ 12H
__ 13H __ 14H __ 15H __ 16H __ 17H __18H __19H $ _____

Total Price — Books and Tapes $ _____

Add $1.00 for orders **under** $10.00
or 10% for orders over $10.00   _____

Enclosed Check or Money Order $_____
(*Please do not send cash*)

Make check payable to: **Lamplight Publications**
             Mail order to: **P.O. Box 3293**
                   Manchester, NH 03105

Please print your name and address **clearly**:

Name _____

Address _____

City _____

State or Province _____

Zip or Postal Code _____

Foreign orders must be submitted in U.S. dollars.
Foreign orders are shipped by uninsured surface mail. We ship all orders within 48 hours of receipt of order.
We will give you a full refund on books and cassette tapes if you are dissatisfied in any way.

Book/Cassette Tape Order Form

To order books and cassette tapes by Jack Hartman, please use this order form:

Books	Qty.	Price
Trust God For Your Finances ($4.95)	_____	$ _____
Nuggets Of Faith ($2.50)	_____	$ _____
Deep Inner Peace ($4.95)	_____	$ _____
How To Study The Bible ($3.50)	_____	$ _____
100 Years From Today ($2.95)	_____	$ _____
Mission Possible ($3.50)	_____	$ _____
Soaring Above The Problems Of Life ($5.95)	_____	$ _____

Cassette Tapes $4.00 ea.
(or $3.00 ea. if three or more tapes are ordered).
Check the tapes that you wish to order.

__ 01H __ 02H __ 03H __ 04H __ 05H __ 06H
__ 07H __ 08H __ 09H __ 10H __ 11H __ 12H
__ 13H __ 14H __ 15H __ 16H __ 17H __18H __19H $ _____

Total Price — Books and Tapes $ _____

Add $1.00 for orders **under** $10.00
or 10% for orders over $10.00   _____

Enclosed Check or Money Order $_____
(Please do not send cash)

Make check payable to: **Lamplight Publications**
          Mail order to: **P.O. Box 3293**
                    Manchester, NH 03105

Please print your name and address **clearly**:

Name _____

Address _____

City _____

State or Province _____

Zip or Postal Code _____

Foreign orders must be submitted in U.S. dollars.
Foreign orders are shipped by uninsured surface mail. We ship all orders within 48 hours of receipt of order.
We will give you a full refund on books and cassette tapes if you are dissatisfied in any way.